How to Start a Law Practice

How to Start a Law Practice

Alexander Y. Benikov

CAROLINA ACADEMIC PRESS
Durham, North Carolina

eISBN 978-1-5310-0035-6

Library of Congress Cataloging-in-Publication Data

Names: Benikov, Alexander Y., author.
Title: How to start a law practice / Alexander Y. Benikov.
Description: Durham, North Carolina : Carolina Academic Press, LLC, 2016. |
   Includes bibliographical references and index.
Identifiers: LCCN 2016036254 | ISBN 9781531000349 (alk. paper)
Subjects: LCSH: Solo law practice--United States.
Classification: LCC KF300 .B46 2016 | DDC 340.068/1--dc23
LC record available at https://lccn.loc.gov/2016036254

Carolina Academic Press, LLC
700 Kent Street
Durham, North Carolina 27701
Telephone (919) 489-7486
Fax (919) 493-5668
www.cap-press.com

Printed in the United States of America
2019 Printing

For My Parents

Contents

Acknowledgments

This book would not have been possible without the help of many amazing people. The first person I have to thank is my amazing wife. She supported my dream when few people did. As I told her on our wedding day, she is my role model. When I was thinking of starting my own practice she was one of the few people who didn't try talking me out of the idea. I also have to thank my parents. I have to thank them for many things, not the least of which was getting me out of the former U.S.S.R. Had my parents not immigrated I would still be living in Russia and my life would be unimaginably different. A big thank you to my whole family is also in order. They have always stood by me and that support has meant the world to me.

A special thank you to Burt Burleson, who was my Law Office Management Professor in law school. He was the first person who got me to seriously think about starting my own practice. Without him I don't know if I would have ever thought about starting my own practice right out of law school. I have to thank Thomas M. Cooley Law School for giving the opportunity to become a lawyer. I also have to thank three amazing college professors that changed the trajectory of my life. Professors Ernie Ettlich, Prakash Chenjeri, and Ken Kempner taught me how to really think, and I will be forever indebted to them.

I also have to thank the many wonderful defense attorneys in Phoenix that took me in under their wing and showed me the ropes and helped me to get on my feet. When I was new to being a lawyer an amazing number of defense lawyers helped me in many different ways. These lawyers showed me the lay of the land and helped me get started. There are too many people to name but they know who they are. The one person I have to mention by name is Jesus Acosta. Jesus was my biggest mentor and I don't know if I would have made it without him.

Lastly I have to thank my amazing publisher, Carolina Academic Press, for taking a chance on my little book.

How to Start a Law Practice

Chapter 1

From the Bakery
to the Courthouse

"Life grants nothing to us mortals without hard work."
— Horace

I share my own story throughout this book, not to brag or to talk about myself, but to hopefully inspire and to motivate law students and young attorneys. I always tell people that if I can do it, you can too. Success in the legal field is about hard work, sacrifice, patience, and perseverance. There are no shortcuts.

In August 2009, I was working in a bakery in South Phoenix, Arizona. I literally had my bar card in my pocket, and I was loading bread trucks in the middle of the night for eight dollars an hour. I would start my shift at two in the morning and finish sometime in the afternoon. I was so tired when I woke up; I once wore two different shoes to work. Most of my co-workers were either recent immigrants or had not finished high school. I was working in the bakery, as it was truly the only job I could find. I had graduated law school, passed the bar, and could not find a job as an attorney. As some of you remember, 2009 was in the middle of what many described as The Great Recession, and unemployment rates were the highest they had been since the 1980s.

Here I was, loading bread trucks in the dead of summer in Phoenix, sweating through my shirt and thinking, "I am a licensed lawyer, why am I working at a bakery?" While studying for the bar, and afterward, I applied for many legal jobs. At first I was picky, later I applied anywhere I could. The one place I really wanted to work was the Public Defender's Office.

I applied at the Maricopa County Public Defender's Office and was interviewed, but was not offered a position. I thought that since I had interned at the Ann Arbor, Michigan, Public Defender's Office, I would likely get hired. Turned out, I was wrong. I had been optimistic about the Public Defender's Office hiring me. I had great letters from judges in Michigan and great letters of recommendation from my bosses in the Michigan public defender's office. None of the letters helped. I had sent out résumés and cover letters to every legal job I could find. I soon lost track of how many résumés I had mailed. I did not receive even one response thanking me for applying. I contacted all of the Cooley Law School alumni that I could find in the Phoenix area. I remember I had a spreadsheet of alumni that I had gotten from Cooley. I went down the list and contacted every single one. I felt like a telemarketer cold-calling people.

Many ignored my phone calls and emails. A few met with me and were helpful and gracious with their time, but no one offered me a job. No one even knew anyone that was hiring. At that time, attorneys that had jobs were thankful to still be employed. One of the alumni that I would later become good friends with told me that he had a pile of over 300 rejection letters when he was looking for work. I knew I was going to be fighting an uphill battle, but I don't think I realized how steep the hill would be. Most law firms were downsizing and laying off attorneys, and here I was trying to land my first legal job.

After I could not find a legal job I began looking for non-legal jobs. At first I was kind of picky about the type of job I wanted. I kept telling myself someone SHOULD give me a good job. I thought I went through all this school, got my Master's and my JD, passed the bar; all this should be enough and I should get a job. I had been in college and law school non-stop for eight years, and now I was done. I thought attending all of that school would ensure a job, but like often before, I was wrong. After a couple of months of not working I began to look for any kind of job I could find.

I began to apply at every place I could. A low point was an interview at a telemarketing/phone scam place by a person with a cross tattoo on his face. He explained that they did not pay for the first month of work but after that the earning potential was limitless. I applied to be a bike-taxi driver and a regular taxi driver. I actually got an interview to sell carpet. I remember how excited I was to get an interview for a minimum wage job because at least they were giving me an interview. Another low point was interviewing at a truck driving school. My interview was in a trailer. The interviewer asked me why I was applying there since I was an attorney. I told him I simply needed a job. I also lied and said I didn't want to be an attorney. I figured it would help my chances of getting hired. It didn't.

Eventually, I learned about an opening at a bakery. The reason I knew of the opening and ultimately got the job was because my friend knew someone that worked there. At orientation I remember the other new hires being very excited because they would be making more than minimum wage. At this point, I was so bummed out from not being able to get a job that I was just happy to be working. I got the job, and I was officially employed as bread-truck loader.

I deeply hated working at the bakery, and continued to send out as many legal résumés as I could. I remember checking various websites all the time in the hoping that a new attorney position would be posted. I posted so many profiles on job websites I often lost track of where I already had a profile and what my password was. While working at the bakery, I began to plan opening my own law practice. I had entertained the idea for a long time and had done a lot of planning. I was also fortunate to have a Law Office Management class in law school.

Over the next several months, the idea of opening my own practice became even more attractive. The more I grew to hate the bakery the more I wanted my own practice. Almost every experienced attorney I spoke to told me that it could not be done, and that I had to work for someone else first. One of the reasons I wanted to write this book is because I could not find anything similar when I needed it. I also wanted to tell young attorneys that opening your own practice right out of law school is possible — incredibly difficult to do, but possible. When I was researching starting my own practice, I looked at a lot of law office management books. I could not find a book called "You Work in a Bakery but You Want to Have Your Own Practice; Here Is What to Do," because that was what I needed. I hope this book will serve as a road map for people who find themselves in a similar position.

After a couple of months at the bakery, management learned that I was an attorney. I was approached and told that they wanted me to stay with the bakery and work my way up the corporate ladder. This was good news. I could literally crawl out from the inside of a bread truck. But, there would be a down side. I would be giving up on a law career for the foreseeable future. I had a choice to make.

I could play it safe and stay at the bakery, or I could open my own law practice. Open a practice in a city where I had zero connections, zero contacts, zero legal experience, zero clients, and zero savings. I quit the bakery on a Friday and started my own practice the following Monday. Starting my own practice was not as scary for me as it may have been for other people for one simple reason. The simple reason is that the odds of me becoming a lawyer in the first place were long at best.

The first time I took the LSAT, I received the lowest score of anyone I had ever met. Today, I joke that I still have the lowest score of any attorney I know. I talk about it like a golf score. "You think yours was low? Ha; let me tell you mine." When I received my score I was shocked. I thought I had done everything right to prep for the test. I had studied, and took a prep class. I took the test seriously, so how did this happen? I remember getting the results right before going on a family vacation. I was so bummed out that the results pretty much ruined that vacation. I also remember thinking that with my score I would never get into law school.

I retook the LSAT and did a little bit better, so I applied to a bunch of different schools that all promptly rejected me. Not one school even wait-listed me. I had been the kid who watched every *Law and Order* episode and told everyone who would listen that I wanted to be a lawyer. In high school I was voted "Most Likely to Become a Lawyer." I had wanted to be a lawyer for as long as I could remember. Now I had to deal with the reality that I would not become a lawyer. When I had pretty much given up on the idea of law school, I was presented an opportunity.

I remember getting a flier from Thomas M. Cooley School of Law and thinking, Is this a real law school? I had never heard of the place. I knew that the school was in Michigan and I knew nothing about Michigan. Not only had I never been to Michigan, but I had never been to the Midwest. I applied because it was my last chance to go to law school, and it was an opportunity to pursue a dream that I had for as long as I could remember. One of the recurring themes of this book is taking advantage of opportunities when they present themselves. Cooley had given me an opportunity.

Cooley accepted me and I was off to Michigan. I moved to Lansing in the dead of winter. I did not know anyone, and it was two days before New Year's Eve. I remember standing on the balcony of my studio apartment in the snow facing the old Oldsmobile plant and thinking this was an ominous sign. For the next three years I would struggle with grades like I never imagined I could. Before this, school had always been fairly easy for me. I had good grades in high school, good grades in undergrad, and very good grades in grad school. I was always able to do well without working very hard.

Now I was studying a ton and having a hard time passing classes. I had heard, like every law student, the old saying that the first year they scare you to death, the second year they work you to death, and the third year they bore you to death. For three years, I felt like I was being worked to death. I studied nonstop but my grades never improved much. Every term I would worry about grades. Each term I knew someone who was getting kicked out because of bad grades. I got one A in law school. It was a one-credit independent study class my last term of my last year. That nicely summarizes my academic life in law school.

I was nearly done with law school and now I had the bar exam to look forward to. At Cooley I took a bar prep course and they showed us a graph. You put in your law school GPA and your LSAT score and it gives you your estimated percentage of passing the bar. I suppose this graph was based on past bar takers. When I plotted my info the graph told me I had a seventeen percent chance of passing. This meant I had an eighty-three percent chance of failing.

As I spent the next several months studying, I kept thinking about the seventeen percent. In a way, knowing about the seventeen percent was a negative because it scared me and put doubt in my head. But, it also helped. It helped because it motivated me to study harder, like the old cliché about how no one believes in you. One of the recurring themes of this book is turning negatives into positives, turning a weakness into strength. I tried to turn the seventeen percent into a positive.

I took studying seriously and tried to take everyone's advice. Anyone that has ever taken the bar loves to give advice. Some of the advice is not great. Some was just plain terrible. One person told me not to study. Some of the best advice that I received is to treat studying as a full-time job. This approach is nothing new, but very valuable nonetheless. Be at your desk on time in the morning and study all day with short breaks. I know for some people studying full-time is not an option, and I understand that.

You have to make time for studying or you are likely to fail. There are a few super-geniuses that can pass without studying. I knew I was not one of those people. My wife, then my girlfriend, was also studying for the bar so she understood what I was going through. Having someone to study with was helpful. Even though we never actually studied together, I liked knowing that I was not going through everything on my own. Every day we complained to each other about how difficult the studying was and every day after complaining we went back to studying. We lived in a small apartment and all we did was study. For nearly three months all we did was study and go to our BARBRI Bar Prep Classes. Long, tedious, and painful story made short — I passed the bar. I had passed by approximately one multiple-choice question, but I passed. I had passed the bar and could not find a job. This brings us back to the bakery.

Why This Book Is Helpful and Different

Lawyers love giving advice. One type of lawyer that loves to give advice more than any other kind of lawyer are the ones that write books telling other new attorneys what to do. Although my goal is the same as anyone that has ever written this type of book, to help new or young attorneys build their own practice and to be professional and ethical in the process, my approach is different.

There are a lot of law office management and practice building books on the market. Many tell you that there is a secret, or a system or tricks to building a practice. Some promise sure fire methods for success. Yet other books feel like an infomercial, which is never good. Authors from Ivy League schools write many law office management books. Authors with very impressive résumés that are as long as a short story write many law office management books. In fact, many of the books are quite good. Many of the books were of great use when I was starting my own practice. My goal here is not to criticize other books. My goal is quite different.

My goal is to offer a book that I wish had been around when I was starting my own practice. A book written by a young lawyer, for young lawyers and law students. A book that is useful, insightful, entertaining, down to earth, and written by someone that not only started their own practice from nothing, but also did not go to a top-tier law school. I went to a law school that is far from an Ivy League law school. Whether I accomplish these goals or not will be for you to decide. Some of my opinions will differ from other attorneys. Remember, often there is more than one correct approach, like the old saying about skinning a cat. Two attorneys can do the same thing in two different ways and both do it correctly.

I will explain my reasoning as I go, and I hope my explanations will be useful to you when it comes time to make these decisions. This book is simple by design. My goal was to write a concise, straightforward text. I have also tried to be honest about the good and the bad in the legal profession. Too many books paint a rosy picture, which is a disservice to young attorneys. I think young attorneys should know not only the benefits of having their own practice, but the drawbacks as well.

There is one last reason this book is different. Many law office management books only give the opinion of the author. I have tried to include approaches and philosophies from a number of excellent attorneys and to combine them in one place. While doing the research for this book, I went to excellent attorneys and asked them their opinions on what new attorneys should know coming into practice. I also asked them what they wish they would have known about the legal profession and running their own office that they know now but didn't know when starting out. I think many of their answers will be valuable to new attorneys. I also spoke to many judges and asked them what they wish young attorneys knew and what they should do when they are starting out. So now I have told you why this book is different. The question you should be asking is, "Why should we listen to you?"

Chapter 2

Why Should I Listen to This Guy? Does He Know What He's Talking About?

Out of necessity, I had to build a law practice from nothing. I didn't set out to build a practice from scratch just to see if I could. I didn't have a choice. I had bills to pay. I also liked to eat and needed money to pay for food. I was tired of the bakery, and I was tired of not getting my phone calls returned from law firms. Looking back, it was amazing how little I knew. In hindsight, not knowing much was a blessing, because I didn't know everything I had ahead of me and what huge challenges I had yet to face.

When I started, I had zero management experience. I had no knowledge of business, managing a business, growing a business, establishing a business, or what it meant to be a business owner. I knew nothing about business. I had never even been an assistant manager at a McDonalds like many of my friends had been. I had read books and articles, but the difference between reading about owning a business and actually running a business is analogous to being chased by a bear as opposed to reading about being chased by a bear. One is scarier than the other.

My lack of business experience was one problem, but it was not my biggest problem. My biggest problem is that I had no real-world legal experience. I say real-world experience because real-world law experience is very different than law school law experience. I had never worked at a firm or an agency. I had volunteered at two firms and interned at the public defender's office, but I had never had an actual legal job. I never second-chaired a trial, never filed a motion, had an office, or prepped a case for trial. I had never met with a client without a supervising attorney present. Not only did I not have any legal work experience, but also I knew nothing about the local legal market. Building a practice while not knowing anything about business was only half of my problem.

Not only was I clueless about how to run a business, I also had no connections to attorneys or judges in the Phoenix area. I didn't have any local attorneys that I could call and ask for help. I had family and friends who were attorneys in Portland, Oregon, and they could help with general questions, but they could do little for local questions. Needless to say, I would be figuring out a lot on my own. Again, the point is not to talk about how I figured out everything out on my own. The point is that I did learn a lot on my own that I hope to pass to others.

There Is No Substitute for Experience

The name of this chapter is, "Why Listen to Me?" One of the biggest reasons I can offer you is experience; in the past four years I have been inside a courtroom practically every single day. Not only have I been in court almost every day, I have also spent a lot of weekends in jail court and in the office. The courts I have practiced in have varied significantly. Some of the courthouses were in Superior Courts, many were in different city courts, some were in Justice of Peace Courts, and some were simply hearing courtrooms. In the past month alone I have appeared in numerous superior courtrooms, two justice courts and seven different municipal courts.

I have dealt with every kind of client, prosecutor, judge, and court staff personality imaginable. I like to think that I learned something from all of them along the way. In those courtrooms I have appeared in front of close to one hundred judges and countless prosecutors. In 2012 alone, I represented 4,500 in-custody defendants. This is not counting out-of-custody defendants or private clients. I have had numerous non-jury trials and dozens of jury trials. I have handled criminal cases, spanning from armed robbery to photo radar tickets, and everything in between.

Another way I learned was by covering other attorneys. Covering is when an attorney pays you to go to court in his place. There are a million reasons why an attorney may need coverage. He may be sick, he may not want to go to court, and he may have a scheduling conflict, or could be on vacation. I will speak more at length about coverage later on. I have covered for over 100 attorneys and learned a lot from them. Some were excellent, some were terrible, and many are in-between.

I have made numerous mistakes along the way and tried to learn from all of them. Some of my mistakes were really little and some were not so little. All attorneys make mistakes and I probably made more than most. I was learning as I went. Often, no one was available to teach me when I was doing something wrong. A lot of the time I would jump into cases that were over my head, kind of like the story of the person who jumps over a ravine and half way over looks down and sees a giant tiger. An important lesson throughout this book is that all attorneys make mistakes. The difference between the good ones and the bad ones is, in part, whether they learn from their mistakes. I see a lot of bad attorneys make the same mistake over and over and never move on.

One last reason I can offer advice is that I have tried to learn from other solo lawyers' mistakes. I have seen more than a couple lawyers fail and I have tried to not repeat their mistakes. I have always felt that learning from other people's mistakes is a lot easier than learning from your own. Many of the mistakes I observed are covered in this book and are easy to avoid if you are careful. New solo practices fail for many of the same reasons that any new business may fail. I will point out many of the pitfalls that new attorneys should watch out for.

Chapter 3

A Few Words on Succeeding in the Legal Profession

Succeeding at running your own practice or establishing a good reputation in the legal profession is no different than succeeding in any field. Some attorneys will tell you how being an attorney is SO different than any other profession. They are right in some ways, but wrong in one big way. The basic principles of success are the same for any profession. Working on achieving excellence is the same no matter if you are a plumber, lawyer, or brain surgeon.

The basic principles are simple. They are principles that you don't need to read in a book to understand. If you asked a sixth grader what it takes to succeed in business, many of them would give you the correct answer. Much of this book is about succeeding in the legal profession and at running your own practice, but the basic principles of success are simple. Work hard (ideally work harder than everyone else), treat people well, be honest, and be patient. The ideas are simple. Like most things however, the difficulty is in execution.

Saying that you should work hard is simple. Everyone says they want to work hard, but many people don't actually want to. Many new attorneys don't want to work weekends, evenings, and holidays. In 2011 and 2012, I worked jail court every major holiday weekend. When I was talking to an attorney who is not known for his work ethic, the subject of me working weekends came up. The other attorney said that he thought it was crappy that I had to work major holidays and that he would not work holidays. I told him that it was not a matter of wanting to work holidays, but a matter of wanting to grow my practice and to make more money . . . so I worked those holidays. A person has to be driven and hard-working to succeed.

Since I started teaching, I have always extended the same invitation to all my students and all the groups I have spoken to. I always invite everyone to come to court to shadow me around. If someone wants to watch a trial, a pretrial, or a hearing, they are always welcome to come. Over the past year I have extended this offer to approximately 300 students.

Out of those 300 about 40 expressed interest in coming to court. Out of those forty, about ten actually came to court once. Out of those ten, one student has come to court with me regularly. She continues to ask me to go to court whenever she can and helps in any way she can. She goes to court without me paying her. She goes to court with me to have the opportunity to learn. Out of all the students I have invited to go to court, guess which student I think will succeed?

No book can teach work ethic and determination. A person is either driven to work hard and succeed or he's not. If a person is driven, he will generally succeed in whatever he is doing. Being driven is more important than being smart. We have all known smart people that were not driven. When I am looking for an attorney or an intern, I will take driven over smart any day. I can teach a person to practice. I cannot teach a person drive and hard work.

You Are Responsible for Your Own Success

Another important lesson on succeeding in the legal profession may seem harsh, but I believe it to be true. No one cares if you succeed or fail. It is your responsibility to succeed. In other words, no one is owed success. This does not mean that you will not have people around that will be helping you, rooting for you, and wanting you to succeed. Obviously, you will have family members, mentors, loved ones, and colleagues that will root for your success. But, ultimately, no one besides you can make you succeed or fail.

The world will keep spinning whether you succeed or fail. I believe it is very important to think actively about the principle that success or failure is dependent on you. If a person begins his career making excuses, those excuses can consume him. When I graduated law school, the unemployment rate was the highest since the 1980s. On top of the bad economy, I had every other challenge facing me that I have already spoken about.

If I had started my practice thinking about how bad the economy was and thinking that if I fail it will be the economy's fault and not my own, this thought process would have only hurt and not helped me. Always remember that you are responsible for the things you can control, like your reputation, and how your peers and clients view you in the legal community.

I see how a negative outlook affects people every day, through my clients and other attorneys. Almost every day I hear from my clients how everything is someone else's fault. Nothing is ever his or her own fault or his or her responsibility. Every day I hear from clients that they can't find a job because the economy is bad, or they can't find a job because the job they want is hard to get, etc. I often think about how these people's lives would be better if they had a different outlook and attitude. Instead of saying, "the economy is bad and I can't find a job," some people thought, "even though the economy is bad I will not give up until I find a job and it's my responsibility to find a job." The job search is just one example, but you get the idea.

Too often, I hear fellow lawyers make excuses why their practice is not doing well or they are not making enough money. Rarely do they examine their attitude and outlook. If these attorneys focused on the positive and not the negative, they would be much happier. This is not to say you should not take outside factors into account. You must have the attitude that you will determine your own future. Obviously, you should think about outside forces like the current economy, but do not let the outside forces determine your outlook and your goals. Another factor that will help to determine if you succeed or fail is how perseverant you are.

As a new attorney, it is important for you to remember that often things will not work the first time you try them. An argument that you may think is great may get shot down at trial. A position that you feel you are qualified for may be given to someone else. You must remember to keep trying and trying and trying. I have a friend who wanted to be a patent attorney. To be a patent attorney you have to take a separate huge exam called The Patent Bar. My friend studied really hard and took the test and failed. He took it again and failed. He took the exam a third and fourth time and failed each time. He did not give up and continued to study and took the exam a fifth time. My friend passed and is now an incredibly successful patent attorney.

Be Careful Where You Get Your Advice

When you are starting out either as a new lawyer working for someone else, or as a new lawyer starting your own practice, every lawyer you meet will try to give you advice. Be careful from whom you take advice. For example, if a lawyer is giving you advice on how to do jury trials but he has not done a jury trial himself in ten years, this should be a red flag. It is important to remember that bad advice is often worse than no advice. As a new lawyer, you will have the problem of often not knowing good advice from bad advice. You must use your own judgment and intuition. The good news is that often the bad advice is so bad it will be easy to spot.

Another common example of lawyers giving new attorneys advice is how to succeed and make lots of money. When I was starting out, a lot of attorneys told me how to build a large, successful practice. The problem was that the lawyers had practices that were barely afloat. I have seen these attorneys who tell me how well they have done for themselves walk out to cars that barely start. My intent is not to imply that young attorneys should not take advice from other attorneys, but be careful whom you listen to.

One good piece of advice, and one that I still use today, is to ask other attorneys if the person giving you advice knows what they are talking about. When I was starting out, I got a lot of trial advice from other attorneys. I would almost always run their advice by one of my mentors to see what they would say. Sometimes they would say it was great advice and that it made sense, so I would listen to that advice. On more than one occasion they told me it was terrible advice, and would explain why it was terrible advice and I would know not to listen to it. Again, when you are new you will not know a lot about the law but always listen to your own intuition. If something doesn't sound right, always listen to your gut.

Be Willing to Work for Free

> "You have to pay the cost to be the boss."
> — Biggie Smalls

When starting out, you must be willing to work for free. There are a couple of reasons why. The first is to get experience. There is no substitute for experience in the legal profession or any profession. One of the best ways to get experience is by offering to work for free. While in law school, I volunteered for two different law offices and learned a lot from both. One of the attorneys was a former prosecutor who taught me a lot about criminal defense. The other lawyer I volunteered for did a little bit of everything, but did not do anything well. I learned a lot of what not do from him. I learned how not to treat your staff or your clients and other valuable lessons. It is very important to remember that you must gain experience any way you can. If someone is willing to pay you to learn that's great, but often it's not very realistic.

The other reason you must be willing to work for free is to show other attorneys that you are serious about building your practice and your career. Even in large markets, the legal community is usually pretty small. In general, bankruptcy attorneys know most other bankruptcy attorneys and criminal defense attorneys know other criminal defense attorneys, etc. The point is that attorneys talk about who the good attorneys are and who the bad attorneys are. By being willing to work for free, you show other attorneys that you are serious about learning your craft and gaining experience. When you talk to most successful attorneys, they will tell you they did more than a little bit of free work for other attorneys when they were starting out.

When I was starting out I did quite a bit of free legal research for other attorneys. Even though I was not getting paid for the work, I was showing those attorneys that I was serious about learning. Today, I have working relationships with many of those attorneys. I also made a lot of court appearances for other attorneys at no charge. One way to look at it is that I was doing free work. I looked at it differently. I looked at it as building relationships and gaining valuable experience. If an attorney or an agency that you respect asks you to help out for free and you say no, they will remember. Building relationships is more valuable than making a quick buck. When I started my own practice, I really wanted to get a contract with the City of Phoenix Public Defender's Office. The City of Phoenix does not have full-time public defenders, but pays private attorneys to handle indigent clients and their criminal matters.

The contracts are very coveted, and there are a lot more applicants every year than there are contracts to be awarded. Almost everyone that has a contract originally started at the county public defender's office or one of the prosecutor agencies, either city or county. I had never worked for an agency so I knew I had to prove myself to get a contract. I think that one of the factors that led to me being awarded a contract so quickly was my willingness to work for the office for free.

Whenever the office called me and asked me if I could fill in, I was always there. Sometimes they could pay me and other times they could not. I never complained and always showed up. Just today as I was writing, the office asked me to fill in. Another attorney was running late as he got stuck in Superior Court. I volunteered to help, because not only is it the right thing to do, it is good for business.

This is just one of many examples that I have had where I was willing to work for free where it benefited my career down the road. The "down the road" part is important. Rarely are there instant payoffs. Also, remember that when you are starting out, you will have plenty of free time on your hands, so it is beneficial to simply help out. In the beginning, you will have the choice of working for free and learning or sitting at home and waiting for the phone to ring.

Networking and Mentors

I don't like the word "networking," but it is an important word. When you are new, you do not have a lot of connections. The way you get access to opportunities is through whom you know. As I have mentioned, many of the best positions, contracts, and opportunities are not advertised. You need to have connections to learn about opportunities. The way you make connections is through networking. Networking does not have to be formal. You don't have to be in a large room with a bunch of people with nametags where everyone introduces him or herself and shares their favorite color.

In all areas, there are events that young attorneys should be attending regularly. There will be state bar conferences and meetings. There will be events for young attorneys and for attorneys in different areas of law. There are events for female attorneys and for minority groups. In Arizona, there are monthly young lawyer events held at restaurants or bars. I always tell my students to go to these events because you never know whom you will meet and what opportunity will be presented to you. I once got a good private client by referral from an attorney I met at a bank get-together.

Many of the best networking opportunities are informal. If you have an opportunity to meet someone, you should do it. When I was new, I would always introduce myself to other attorneys. I would tell them that I was new and often strike up a conversation. Some of these conversations resulted in coverage jobs for me. Sometimes the attorneys themselves didn't need coverage but they knew someone who did. More than once I've received a phone call from an attorney telling me they heard about me from another attorney.

If there is an attorney you want to learn from, invite them to lunch or coffee. Some will say no, and you have lost nothing. I have invited many attorneys to lunch or to coffee that have not responded. Some of the best connections I have made, however, were from inviting other attorneys to coffee or lunch. Whether you are in a firm or on your own, you will need a mentor or mentors.

Having a good mentor can have a huge impact on your career. Not only can a good mentor enhance your career, the relationship can determine whether your practice succeeds of fails. If you are at firm, finding a mentor should not be very difficult; there will be people at the firm. If the firm is large, you will have a supervising attorney or someone actually assigned to you as a mentor. If you are on your own, it will be up to you to find a mentor.

I have had many mentors, but one to whom I owe the most. I met him at a young-lawyer event. I introduced myself and invited him to lunch. After lunch, I asked him if I could go to court with him to learn. I started going to court with him and I went often. I would call him almost every evening and see what he had on his schedule the following day. I spent several months following him around and learning a ton. Following him around had two benefits. I was learning from him, but he was also introducing me to people. He would say that I was new and if anyone needed coverage to call me. All my first coverage clients came about from this experience. If it were not for him, I am not sure if my practice would have survived. I was lucky and fortunate to find a great mentor.

Like with everything, luck favors the motivated. If I had not asked to come to court and taken it upon myself to come, nothing good would have resulted from the meeting. Always remember that you need the mentor much more than they need you. When offering your services to someone, it is on you to convince the person why they should let you help them. Be willing to do free legal research or free coverage. Make sure the attorney you want to work with knows that you are willing to help. You must be willing to prove yourself.

There is an *Entourage* episode where an assistant is trying to get promoted to an agent. The assistant's boss makes him sit outside the house until the middle of the night. The reason the assistant has to sit outside for half the night is to show the boss that he is committed and willing to do anything to get the promotion. Young attorneys must also be willing to do anything to show their mentors that they are serious. My mentor knew that he could call me at any time and I would make myself available to help in any way that I could.

I have had many people say they wanted to come to court with me only to blow me off at the last minute. I have had people not show up at all. As soon as someone has not shown up for court and not taken the time to text me or email me, there is zero chance that I will invite them to shadow me again. Most attorneys want to be helpful to young attorneys, but no one likes having their time wasted. You must demonstrate that you are serious. One of the ways you demonstrate you are serious is by contacting a prospective mentor more than once.

I have a good attorney friend that I met because he was a Cooley alumnus. I found him on the alumni database and we exchanged a couple of emails before I moved to Arizona from Michigan. When we met for lunch once I moved, he told me something that really stuck with me. He told me that he had a lot of Cooley grads reach out to him and want to meet him. He told me that they had to reach out to him more than once. He told me if someone reached out to him once, or had lunch with him once he didn't really remember them and wouldn't do a lot for them. I now have students and alumni reaching out to me and I do the same thing. I want to know someone is committed and devoted to succeeding before I go out of my way to help them. Why would I help someone who is not serious about helping himself?

Chapter 4

The Legal Profession is Changing

This should not come as a shock to anyone. Entire books have been written on how the profession is changing. Everything from how law schools teach students to how firms are run is in a state of flux. My goal for this chapter is to quickly point out several ways the profession is changing, and why. One of the biggest changes is that there are more lawyers and fewer jobs. More and more people are going to law school, while at the same time, the bad economy and other factors are affecting the legal job market. A simple supply and demand analysis shows us that there is a higher supply of lawyers than a demand for them.

What this means for any new attorney is that they must be more creative, flexible, and willing to adapt to survive. The old way of looking at things will no longer work. Things that have worked in the past may not work now for a variety of reasons. One of my biggest goals for this book is to get law students and recent law school graduates to start thinking outside the box (pardon the cliché). New attorneys must evolve past the old ways of doing things. Like all species, attorneys must evolve. Young attorneys must be creative in how they run their practices and how they grow their practices.

For better or worse, the old-school model of graduating law school, easily finding a job, and staying with one firm your entire career is generally not realistic anymore. Many young attorneys hope that their career will start like the opening of the movie based on John Grisham's *The Firm*, where Tom Cruise receives lots of offers from top firms and gets to choose which job to take. New lawyers must evolve to survive. Think of the dinosaurs, who, unfortunately, are not with us anymore. There are still some attorneys who graduate and easily find work, but this is becoming the exception. I am a big believer in hoping for the best but preparing for the worst. If you graduate and easily find a great job, that is great, but what if you don't, then what? The stark reality is that more students than not do not have work lined up when they graduate.

How people receive legal services is also changing. There are more document preparation services, paralegals, and websites that are taking work away from attorneys. Most of us have seen the billboards or newspaper ads saying "DIVORCE FOR $200" or something similar. If you are looking to get a divorce you have several options. You can go to a traditional divorce/family law lawyer who tells you they can do your divorce for several thousand dollars. Or, you can have a document prep place do your divorce for $200. As a consumer, the $200 place is tempting.

Part of the reason that the document preparation place is tempting is because people, usually wrongly, believe they can solve their own legal problems and don't need the services of an attorney. Even though no one would ever attempt to do their own surgery to save money by not paying a surgeon, people will try to handle their own legal matter to save money on paying a lawyer. Online legal service providers have also cut into how much work lawyers have.

Much like the $200 divorce, many of us have seen ads for web services that say you don't need to pay a high-priced attorney and can do everything on your own with their help for a fraction of the price. Between do-it-yourself law books, document prep places, and online legal services, it is becoming harder and harder for attorneys to get clients.

Although how people get legal services is changing, law firms themselves are also changing. Today, it is hard to go a week without seeing a story about some mega-firm filing for bankruptcy or dissolving and leaving everyone out of work. There was a time that once you got hired at a big prestigious firm, you had job security for life. That time is largely gone. In 2012, one of the largest law firms in the world with over 1,300 partners filed for bankruptcy.[1] Can you imagine being one of the 1,300 attorneys? You worked hard, got a job at a great firm, and thought you would be at that firm for a long time. You put your entire life into that firm, often devoting time to the firm at the cost of health, family, and relationships. Then, one perfectly good day you get an email or a phone call that the firm is closing and that you are out of work.

Unfortunately for young attorneys, huge firms closing is not as rare as one would think or hope. The reasons large firms go out of business are beyond the scope of this book, but the point is that there is less job security in large firms than there used to be, and young or new lawyers must be prepared for this. Again, hope for the best, but prepare for the worst.

---

1. http://www.forbes.com/sites/danielfisher/2012/05/29/dewey-leboeuf-bankruptcy -a-one-off-but-still/.

There are not only fewer "big law" jobs than in the past but there are more and more attorneys starting their own practices. Attorneys that in the past would have been at a firm or a government agency may have to start their own practice, as they have no choice. What this means is that there are more attorneys competing over the same clients. So where in the past there might have been 10 lawyers competing over 100 clients now there are 100 lawyers competing over those same 100 clients.

A fun exercise is to Google your hometown and the type of law that you are interested in. For example, Google "Phoenix and Business Lawyer." You will be amazed by how many lawyers there are, all competing over the same clients. I practice criminal law exclusively in the Phoenix area and it seems like every day I meet another attorney that is hanging his or her own shingle and hoping to practice criminal law. There is no reason to think that more and more attorneys competing over the same clients is likely to change any time soon.

Another change that is happening is how people perceive lawyers. I would equate the change with how people viewed politicians in the past versus how politicians are viewed today. From what I understand when someone used to aspire to be a politician it was considered a noble calling and was respected by the public. Today if someone says they are a politician, thoughts of corruptions, selfishness, and not getting anything done probably come to mind. Lawyers face a similar problem.

In 2012, Gallup looked at how people view the trustworthiness of different professions and asked the following question: "please tell me how would you rate the honesty and ethical standard of people in these different fields — very high, average, low or very low."[2] Not surprisingly, professions like nursing and medical doctors were ranked as very trustworthy. Lawyers were ranked as some of the least ethical and least professional.[3] The poll also showed that people have been trusting lawyers less and less ever since the poll was first done in 1974.[4] In general, lawyers are not viewed as problem solvers and helpers. Many more people today view them as causing problems. There are several reasons for the change.

I think one of the big reasons for the negative way lawyers are viewed is that many people don't understand what lawyers actually do. I deal with a lot of

---

2. www.gallup.com/poll/1654/honesty-ethics-professions.aspx
3. *Id.*
4. *Id.*

people that don't understand what it is I do as a criminal defense attorney. I often have people ask me how I feel about getting guilty people out of prison and away from responsibility for their actions. As a defense attorney you become accustomed to the phrase "get a defendant off," instead of phrases like "protecting people's rights" and "defending liberty."

Almost every defense attorney has, at one point or another, been asked how they can do what they do. The not-so-subtle implication being that our work is so horrible, a normal person would never want to do it. Many of us heard the horrible phrase that a lawyer "got someone off on a technicality." That technicality is the Constitution of the United States, but I digress.

Part of the problem is that most non-lawyers blame lawyers for the actions of the lawyer's clients. Just because a criminal defense attorney represents someone charged with some horrible crime obviously doesn't mean that that lawyer endorses the actions of his client. The same principle is true in civil cases. When a client asks a lawyer to help with a cause that is important to the client but not to the lawyer, it does not mean that the lawyer is endorsing that issue.

One example that comes to mind is when ACLU was defending the North American Man Boy Love Association. What the ACLU was defending was the First Amendment and not what NAMBLA stood for, but many people blamed the lawyers of the ACLU for representing such a despicable group. Fighting for the First Amendment and other worthy causes often means that lawyers have to represent unpopular causes as a way to defend liberties that everyone values.

There are also many smaller scale examples where a lawyer is doing what their client wants them to do. Blaming an attorney for doing what their client wants would be like blaming a house painter when the owner picks out a really ugly color for their houses.

How the media portrays lawyers hasn't helped either. In almost any movie or TV show where there is an attorney, the chances are that the attorney is portrayed as unethical or underhanded or not trustworthy. Most lawyers in movies or TV shows are somewhere between shifty and evil. Modern shows, such as *The Sopranos, Boston Legal, Sons Of Anarchy, The Wire,* and *Breaking Bad,* all have attorneys that lie, do unethical things, and are portrayed in a bad light.

Breaking Bad features an attorney that is not only unethical but is actively involved in helping his clients commit crime. The attorney not only constantly lies but also often goes behind his client's back to reveal confidential information. When I teach Professional Responsibility, I often play clips of the show and tell my students to do the opposite of what the attorney does to comply with the Model Ethical Rules. Even though most people watching the show know to some extent that the character is a comedic fictional character, I think many people watching think the character is just an exaggerated version of what real defense lawyers are like.

While thinking about this chapter, I tried to think of popular movies or TV shows that depict attorneys in a positive light. I was trying to think of examples where lawyers are ethical and do the right thing, but I could not come up with many examples. All this goes to show that new or young attorneys must work that much harder to show that real attorneys are ethical and honest so that attorneys can begin to work towards restoring a positive image. Young and new attorneys must remember that they represent an entire profession whether they want to or not. Every time one lawyer is dishonest or unethical it reflects poorly on the entire profession. New and young attorneys must never forget this.

The last major reason for why attorneys are viewed as unethical is what the public perceives as "frivolous lawsuits." Chances are that when an attorney tells someone what they do, one of the first questions that will get asked is about "frivolous lawsuits" and how attorneys are allowed to represent people in these cases. One of the most famous cases that attorneys are commonly asked about is the McDonald's hot coffee case.

Many of you know about this case, but for those that don't, it involved a woman spilling hot coffee on her lap and suing the restaurant for the coffee being too hot.[5] The jury found for the woman and gave her $200,000 in actual damages. The reason the case made news was because the jury also awarded 2.7 million dollars to the plaintiff. There was a lot of national coverage of the story and people were outraged that someone would get so much money for spilling coffee on her. There was a lot of information that people did not know about the case, which would probably change their views. According to reports:

> The sweatpants Liebeck was wearing absorbed the coffee and held
> it next to her skin. A vascular surgeon determined that Liebeck suf-
> fered full thickness burns (or third-degree burns) over 6 percent of
> her body, including her inner thighs, perineum, buttocks, and geni-
> tal and groin areas. She was hospitalized for eight days, during which

---

5. http://www.lectlaw.com/files/cur78.htm

time she underwent skin grafting. Liebeck, who also underwent debridement treatments, sought to settle her claim for $20,000, but McDonalds refused.[6]

While researching the infamous case I saw the pictures of the burns caused by the hot coffee. The pictures were truly terrible to look at as large parts of the flesh had melted off. Most people did not know that there had been hundreds of complaints against McDonalds for their coffee being too hot. Many people did not know that McDonalds had a policy of keeping their coffee very hot, had discussed the issue, and chosen to not address the problem.[7] Lastly, 2.7 million dollars sounds like a lot of money, but it is the amount that McDonalds makes off coffee in two days. The amount of punitive damages was later reduced to $480,000 dollars by the court.[8] The point is that many people think of attorneys as taking on these "frivolous" lawsuits even though they are often serious.

---

6. http://www.lectlaw.com/files/cur78.htm
7. http://www.lectlaw.com/files/cur78.htm
8. http://www.lectlaw.com/files/cur78.htm

Chapter 5

Should You Start Your Own Practice?

Having your own practice can be the best thing in the world. For me, the advantages far outweigh the disadvantages. There are many advantages and some disadvantages, and I'll talk about them in more detail in a bit. Having your own practice is not for everyone. This is incredibly important and worth repeating. Having your own practice is NOT for everyone. The logical question is who should and should not have their own practice. First, who should not start their own practice?

When you are deciding on whether or not you should start your own practice you MUST be honest with yourself. If you are not self-motivated you should not have your own practice. If you are averse to all risk you should not have your own practice. There is obvious risk in starting your own practice. The practice could fail. If you do not address this reality, you are not being honest with yourself.

If you prefer just getting a paycheck for your work and do not want all the responsibility on you, you should not have your own practice. If you are painfully shy and want to avoid client interaction you should not start your own practice. It is worth mentioning that there are plenty of excellent lawyers that have no interest in having their own practice and there is nothing wrong with this. Some attorneys do not want the headache of dealing with running the business, some have found great bosses and do not want to leave and obviously there is nothing wrong with this. I know many excellent attorneys that have chosen to spend their entire careers at a government agency. Some attorneys are perfectly happy not having their own practice and not being in the private sector. Again, the key is that you have to be honest with yourself and what you want.

That being said, you may not know what you want right away and this is okay too. I meet a lot of students who for example, say they want to be prosecutors until they spend a day with me or a different defense attorney in court and suddenly they don't want to be prosecutors anymore. Some people think they want to have their own practice until they realize all the planning, managing, and organizing that goes into it, and then they want to work for someone else.

I have developed a simple test for deciding if you should have your own practice. Ask yourself if you are willing to outwork everyone. If the answer is yes, you should think about having your own practice. If the answer is no, you should not have your own practice. If you are willing to wake up earlier, stay at work longer and out-hustle other attorneys you should think about having your own practice. If you decide to have your own practice the next factor to think about is timing.

Timing

One of the hardest decision facing attorneys is when to start their own practice. Should they do it right away, wait a couple of years, or wait more than a couple of years? Obviously, there are different opinions and philosophies. A common and traditional view is that it is a good idea to work for someone else for a couple of years, and then start your own practice. There are advantages to this model but also several hidden risks.

The major advantage is that someone takes you under his wing and teaches you the ropes. Someone teaches you how to prepare documents and motions, how to go to court, and how to handle clients and their problems. Like a good mentor, they slowly bring you up and you learn as you go while earning a living. This is all great-sounding, but there are several hidden risks that many, if not all, new attorneys do not think about.

Say, for example, you get a job at a firm or an agency and the place is terrible. Every term, I see my law students take jobs with firms that I know are disreputable, dishonest, and will teach the students terrible habits. The problem is that with the students being new attorneys, they do not know that what they are learning is wrong. New attorneys often wrongly assume that just because they are learning they are automatically learning the correct way of doing things. For attorneys, as in any profession, is it very difficult to unlearn bad habits and virtually impossible to undo a bad reputation. This point brings us to the next hidden danger of working for someone else.

If you are a new attorney and you get a job for a bad firm, you might figure it's OK because I am a good attorney and I am honest and my reputation will be good. You figure the place you work at has a less-than-stellar reputation, but your own personal reputation will not be affected. The problem with this is that whether it is fair or not, an attorney takes on the reputation of the place where he or she works. If you work for a terrible or dishonest firm, other attorneys will associate the bad traits of that firm with you.

I know several very good attorneys at bad firms and I know the reputation of those attorneys has suffered as a result of where they work. As I have mentioned and will continue to mention, your reputation is the single most important thing you have as an attorney. Unfortunately, there are other hidden dangers when you work for someone else.

Say you have found a great job, your mentor is great, the firm has a great reputation, and you have learned a lot. Two or three years go by and you decide you want to go out on your own. You have about twenty or thirty of your own clients that you have brought to the firm and you figure the clients will go with you to your new solo firm. You go to your boss and say thanks for everything; I am leaving and taking my clients with me. Your boss says great, good luck, but the clients belong to the firm and if you try taking them we will sue you into nonexistence. This actually happened to an attorney friend of mine. She left one firm and tried to take her clients to her new firm and the old firm sued her and it has been a huge strain on her.

When I started my practice I had no clients, but I always knew that the clients that I got were my own and not the firm that I was working for. Remember that it's better to have a few clients that are yours than to have many clients, of whom zero are yours. This is something to think about, because if you leave a firm and you are not allowed to take any of the firm's clients, how will you make money? This brings us to the last hazard of working for someone else before starting your own practice.

Say you have been working for one or several firms for five or seven or ten years. Things are going well and you are thinking of starting your own practice. You may have one or two kids that you did not have when you finished law school. You have a mortgage and are used to a certain lifestyle. An attorney in this scenario may be used to certain vacations, cars and other things (think of lawyer stereotypes such as golf club memberships).

Say you are making $100,000 a year. You want to leave your job because maybe you don't like the work, or your bosses, or the firm structure, or for whatever reason. The problem is that many attorneys in such scenarios realize that they cannot afford to leave. They realize that, in many ways, they would be starting over if they went out on their own. Many attorneys get stuck at firms under similar circumstances.

Many attorneys working for government agencies get stuck in a similar problem that has to do with their pensions. "Golden handcuffs" is an expression that most government attorneys are familiar with and works like this: a government attorney usually must stay at an agency for a certain number of years before her pension vests. So first the attorney must stay at an agency for a certain number of years, often five years. Next, attorneys are often worried that if they leave they will not get an actual retirement. Some attorneys end up spending their entire careers at an agency that they might have otherwise left, because the pension is so important to them.

For the above reasons I am an advocate of people starting their own practices sooner rather than later. When I decided to start my own practice I figured it would take me about three years to establish. I was twenty-seven at the time, and I figured if I could have a running practice by the time I was thirty, I would be happy. I also figured, and I think most attorneys would agree, that it is easier to fail when you are young than when you are older.

Let's look at our example of the attorney at the firm making $100,000 a year. If my practice had failed, I would have been out a couple thousand dollars, but not much else. If the experienced attorney fails she may lose her house, her cars, and jeopardize her entire lifestyle and the future of her children. The stakes of me failing when I started were so much lower because I had less to lose; I had no money or house, so it took some of the pressure off me when I did start.

I can't tell anyone when the perfect time to start his or her own practice is, but I can tell you I have never met an attorney that regretted going out on his own. I can also tell you that I have spoken to many attorneys that eventually went out on their own and wish they had done it sooner for many of the reasons above. One attorney comes to mind. He is one of the best criminal defense attorneys in town and spent close to fourteen years working for other attorneys. He told me that he always wanted to go out on his own but had children and was worried. He told me that once he finally did go out on his own he was mad he didn't do it much sooner.

So when is the best time to go out on your own? There is no simple answer. Ideally, you can get some experience working for someone else and then go out on your own. Later on, I will argue that for some people going out on their own right out of law school can be a good idea, but it is not for everyone.

Advantages and Disadvantages of Having Your Own Practice

One of the biggest advantages to working for yourself is that you work for yourself. It is hard to describe how nice it is not having a boss. All of us have had bosses and a good boss can be pleasant to work for. Most of us have also had terrible bosses, and I have had more than my fair share. Even if you are fortunate to have a good boss, you are still answering to someone else. Someone above you is making decisions for you. For some people, this is not a problem, but for me, having the opportunity to work for myself was always very enticing.

There are many benefits that people may not initially think of. For me, being able to go on vacation or to take a day off is priceless. As I am writing this chapter, it is a Thursday and I did not have any court appearances so I stayed home and did what I wanted to do. I didn't have to check in with my boss and ask if I could stay home. Being able to go on vacation when I want and not having to ask permission is also valuable. I have known more than a few attorneys who had planned vacations only to have those plans ruined by their boss at the last minute.

Your boss walks into your office and says he needs you to work next week. You tell him you have been looking forward to an amazing trip with your family for a year. Your boss tells you that you can look forward to looking for work if you don't show up next week, end of conversation. I am able to take all the vacations and trips that I want. Obviously, I know that if I am out of town I am not making money, but the decision is mine and that's the whole point.

Another advantage is that you decide what direction your practice will take. When I started taking on major felonies cases I didn't have to run the idea by my boss to get his permission. Also, when I gave up my old office I didn't have to ask anyone permission. Having control over little things is nice, but having control over larger decisions is the real benefit. When I decided I wanted to devote more of my time to teaching there was no approval from my boss that I had to get, because I don't have a boss.

If I ever decided that I wanted to work part time, for example, the decision would be mine and no one else's. If I ever decided that I didn't want to do criminal defense work and wanted to do something completely different I could. Try going to your boss at a bankruptcy firm and tell him you want to start doing nothing but environmental protection work. The last point transitions into the next benefit, which is job security.

I will never get fired and I know this for a fact. For me, this has great value. My practice may slow down or I may have fewer clients. I may choose to close my practice or my practice could go out of business but I will never have someone walk into my office and tell me that I longer have a job with a firm. If you are the new attorney at a firm and times get tough, the firm has to cut costs . . . guess who is getting fired? In this recent economy, many firms have downsized and entire departments have been laid off.

Living in Arizona, I know of firms laying off their entire real estate departments. I know of attorneys having little or no notice before being fired. A partner at a firm is never going to lay herself off; they will always find someone below them on the corporate ladder. Again, with my own practice I know there will be good years and slow years, but I will never get fired.

What attracted me the most to having my own practice is also potentially the biggest drawback. I loved that I was starting with nothing and trying to grow something from scratch. Some people would view this as a negative. It's obviously harder to build something from nothing as opposed to something from something. I loved knowing that I am solely responsible for the success of my practice.

If I bring in a big client or a big case, the entire reward goes to me and no one else. There is nothing wrong with not wanting to build your own business. As I mentioned earlier, you must be honest with yourself when deciding if you want to have your own practice. If building something out of nothing does not appeal to you, having your own practice is not for you.

I never liked the idea that when you work for a firm, ultimately you are making money for someone else. Even though the firm may be paying you a decent salary, this doesn't change the fact that someone above you is making more money than you off of your hard work. Some people are not bothered by this concept, but I am.

The issue is not only about money, but also reputation. If you work hard and do all the right things, the firm you work for benefits from your work. I like the idea of the rewards of my hard work going to me and no one else. This may sound selfish, but to me it's not about selfishness but about the person who did the work getting the reward. The beauty is in the simplicity. If you run a good practice you do well; if you don't run a good practice, you don't do well.

I still have a lot of days that I have a hard time believing that I get to do what I do for a job. I really like what I do and I love working for myself. I love going on vacation when I want to, I love the flexibility, and I love knowing that I am building something out of nothing. There are obviously many advantages to having your own practice, but I would be dishonest if I did not talk about the disadvantages. Some of the disadvantages I knew about before starting my own practice, others I have learned about along the way.

Advantages of Working for a Firm and Disadvantages of Working for Yourself

Having your own practice is not for everyone, and you have to be honest with yourself if it is something for you. One of the advantages of working for someone else is the support that is available to you. Just today I was talking to an attorney about how I was having a problem with my QuickBooks accounting software. He told me his firm had a person that did all the billing and finance. Since I work for myself, I do all the accounting myself. I do everything on my own, which cuts down on overhead but increases the responsibilities I have to worry about, whereas someone at a firm generally only has to focus on clients.

Having a person do all of the finance work is one advantage of working for someone else and just one example of the benefits you get at a firm that you normally don't have when you are on your own. I could go out and hire someone to do all my finances, but that would cut into my profit and for me it's not worth hiring someone. Firms may offer logistical support such as an assistant, help with research, and other services. I know many large firms have their own print department for making document copies and transcripts.

Medium or large firms may offer other benefits that a solo practice may not. Firms often offer benefits ranging from health insurance to retirement, to name just two. I know several attorneys at large firms that have expense accounts for cell phones, trips, lunches, dinners, and other fun incidentals. I know one attorney that told me that when he was at a large firm and he had to work during the evening, the firm would pay for take-out from any restaurant in the city and have the food delivered to the office. The same attorney told me that he had several paid trips to conferences. If having some of the benefits I spoke about is important to you, working for a large- or medium-size firm may be for you.

For some attorneys, the prestige of working for a large firm is important. For some people, being associated with a big firm or a fancy firm name is important, and a big part of their identity. I have met many of these attorneys and they can't wait to tell you where they work. For many of these people, being associated with a prestigious firm means they are successful attorneys. Being at a big, reputable firm does not mean that an attorney is necessarily competent or skilled, but to some people it is important. If having the safety net of a big firm is important, perhaps having your own firm is not for you.

One of the other disadvantages of having your own practice versus working for a firm or agency is that there are many ethical pitfalls that a young or inexperienced attorney can fall into. There are several reasons a solo attorney may be more at risk. The first reason is that when you are on your own there is no one checking your work. You can have another attorney look over your work, but realistically you won't have someone else checking all of your work like you might at a firm.

Another reason solo attorneys are more at risk is that many, if not all, large firms have an entire department or boards or committees devoted to ethics. If an attorney is not sure how to go about doing something, he can go to the person or committee at the firm and get the answer. For obvious reasons, this is a definitive advantage of being at a firm. One last ethical disadvantage of being in a solo practice arises if the solo attorney is new and not experienced.

When an attorney is new, it is often difficult to know what the ethical rules say about a certain issue or how to deal with a specific situation. As an attorney becomes more experienced he has the same situations arise over time and it becomes easier to deal with situations when they come up. As with any anything, the more you do something the easier it becomes. At a firm you can go to a different attorney or your supervising attorney and get guidance on an ethics questions or a situation, whereas when you are a solo attorney you are more or less on your own.

Lack of funding can be another major disadvantage of being solo as opposed to working at a firm. One of the main reasons any new business fails is a lack of capital, as well as underestimating how much money a business will need to get by. A law practice is no different in that it needs capital to survive. This book will cover firm funding at length later on, but you don't need a business degree to know that money will have to come from somewhere.

When a practice is started, the person starting it must know that if he does not have enough money to keep the lights on the business will be forced to close. The obvious advantage of being at a firm is that someone has already built the firm. When you take a job at a firm you are stepping into something that has already been built. You not only have access to all of the firm's resources, but you don't have to worry about the firm running out of money and having your office on a street corner. This is another place where knowing yourself is very important. Are you good at managing money? Are you good at budgeting and planning? If not, how realistic is it for you to manage your firm's finances. The formula is simple, if more money goes out than comes in: GAME OVER.

One last disadvantage that is important to discuss has to do with isolation and a lack of contact with other attorneys. When you are at a firm you are around other people. At a firm there are other associate attorneys, managing attorneys, paralegals, assistants, tech support people and all the other people you see at an office. Everyone interacts, and friendships and relationships are formed. When you are a solo attorney you are on your own.

If you spend a lot of time in court, as I do, you see other attorneys, but you still spend most of your time on your own in an office or at home. Many attorneys now work from home and may feel isolated. Many attorneys do not mind being on their own, but it's still worth thinking about. I like being around other attorneys, but I also like being on my own, so working by myself is not a problem. I also share an office with two other attorneys, which helps. Office-sharing arrangements will be discussed at length later on. If being around other people is important to you, a firm or an agency job may be worth thinking about. There are ways to establish networks to combat a feeling of isolation.

Technology has helped attorneys stay in touch. Many attorneys belong to listservs where ideas and thoughts are exchanged. There are many different types of listservs. Some are geared for one type of law, while others are geared for a type of practice. For example, there may be a listserv for bankruptcy attorneys or criminal defense attorneys. There are also listservs for solo practitioners.

Some of the listservs are local while others are national or regional. Some of the lists are open to everyone, while others are by invitation only. Like everything, some of the lists are more useful than others. Some are nothing more than a place for attorneys to gossip, while some are wonderfully useful for motions, ideas, and discussions.

Chapter 6

So You've Decided to Start Your Own Practice — Now What?

Where to Locate Your Practice

This seems like an obvious question, but it is an important one. If you are in a location that you like, you should stay there. The decision is harder if you are in geographic location where the economy is bad. I went to law school in Michigan and I knew that if I had stayed in Michigan it would have been harder to start my practice there. It is no secret that Michigan's economy is not doing very well. Starting any business in an economically depressed area makes it that much harder. I understand some people are not able to move for different reasons. If you are in a position where you can move and want to move, it is at least something to think about.

Sometimes you will be better off if you move to a different location. There are several scenarios where you might want to think about moving. You might be in a small town where there is not a big need for attorneys. You may be in a town with a bad economy. Another option is that you simply want to move; there is nothing wrong with this. When deciding if you should move to a different area to practice, there are several things to consider.

The main thing to think about is where you will most likely be happy. The main reason you should be starting your own practice is because you think you will be happier working for yourself. If you are not happy with where you are located you will never be happy. This is not a difficult concept. If you hate the cold, you should not start your practice in Minnesota. If you hate humidity, Florida is probably not for you. I use the weather as an example, but there are many factors to consider.

Remember that there is at least one downside to starting somewhere new, and I know this firsthand. When you move somewhere new you don't have any contacts. You generally will not have any work contacts or personal contacts. When my wife and I moved to Arizona, we knew we would be starting from scratch. We were OK with starting over because we wanted to live in

Arizona. If you are not in a city you want to be in, you will have to decide if moving is worth it. For us it was worth it and we are glad we did. I have a very good friend who came to my Law Office and Management class and told my students they should move to where the jobs are. I think my friend makes a good point. Think of where the jobs are and where you will be happy and move if you need to.

If you are going to move to a different city there are a number of factors to consider. For example:

- Proximity to family (if you want to be close to family, not everyone does)
- Strength of the local job market (is the city in an economically depressed area?)
- Number of attorneys already in the area (the more people practicing the more competitive the market will be)
- How much you like/dislike the city (you want to be somewhere where you will be happy)
- The affordability of the city (or lack of affordability)
- Will your husband/wife like the city (if your significant other is not happy, how likely are you to be happy?)?
- Is this a place you want to be in for a long time (moving cities is not easy)?

One example of how where you live makes a big difference is one of my friends from law school. When he graduated he chose to stay in Michigan. As I write this in 2013 it is no secret that the Michigan economy is struggling and jobs are hard to find. As of August 2013 the unemployment rate in Michigan was nine percent.[1] After not being able to find work for a long time he found work as a prosecutor making about $40,000 dollars. A comparable job in Maricopa County, Arizona, pays about $60,000 dollars. That is a huge difference in salary. Over five years the Arizona job will pay $100,000 more than the Michigan job.

One Field or Many Fields of Law?

One of the first decisions you will have to make is if you are going to focus on one type of law or practice several different types. Obviously there are advantages and disadvantages to both. The advantage to practicing several areas of law is that you will be more marketable to clients. If someone comes to you to do a business contract and then needs someone for a divorce, and you practice both, you have gained two cases out of one client. When you only practice one area of law you will often have to turn potential clients away.

---

1. http://www.bls.gov/eag/eag.mi.htm

When a client asks you if you can help with his case and that case is an area of law you don't practice, that is money walking out your door.

Another advantage to practicing more than one area of law is that there is more variety to your work. Some people don't mind doing the same type of work over and over, but the more areas of law you practice in, the bigger the range there will be in your work. If you decide to practice more than one area of law, you have to then decide if you will do a little of everything or focus on two or three areas of law. Some areas make sense to do together.

For example, in Phoenix it makes sense for someone to practice immigration law and criminal law, as the two are often related. One of the attorneys in my office has built a successful immigration practice after initially only doing criminal work. He realized that many of the clients he was representing in criminal matters needed help with their immigration matters as well.

My friend realized that he could turn away a lot of work or he could learn immigration law and keep the clients. Now he benefits from his knowledge in two ways. He is not only able to help his criminal clients with immigration matters, but he can also help his immigration clients with criminal matters. My friend was able to build a successful practice doing two types of law and I think two is the most someone can practice while still having a mastery of those areas.

Today the law and the practice of law are more complex than ever. A competent attorney must stay up to date on current cases, court trends, case trends, and so on. A competent attorney must attend seminars and continuing legal education seminars to stay current. For example, in Arizona the DUI laws change almost every year. The amount of mandatory jail, fees, and interlock requirements all change and a competent attorney must stay on top of all the changes. All fields of law are in a constant change of flux. I think an attorney can stay current on two fields of law at most. I think practicing three areas is possible, but I would not suggest more than two.

My personal opinion is that new attorneys starting their own practice should focus on one area of law. There are several reasons I believe it is best to focus on one area of law. First, when you are new there is very little that you know and much more that you don't. I think it's easier and a more efficient use of your time to attempt to master one field of law. I have been practicing nothing but criminal law for close to four years now and I still feel there are a ton of things I don't know.

Second, solo attorneys are better off focusing on one area of law because today most clients want to go to an attorney that focuses one area of law. In other words, most clients want a specialist. Think of it as looking for a doctor. You need surgery and you have to find a doctor to perform the surgery. Do you want to go to a general practitioner who does a little bit of surgery, or would you rather go to a surgeon who does nothing but the exact surgery that you need? I have had more than a few clients tell me that the reason they hired me was because I practice nothing but criminal law, as opposed to a different attorney that does a little bit of everything.

I chose to focus on criminal law right from the start. I wanted to learn the field well and focus my attention and energy on learning one thing thoroughly. I knew that by focusing on one area of law I would be losing some potential clients who would want to hire me for something else. Over the years I have had potential clients come to me for personal injury cases or civil work, and I have told them that I only do criminal work. When you are new and in need of work it is hard to turn away paying clients, but I wanted to stick with my plan and focus on one area.

Criminal law, like all fields of law, has a lot of variety within the field, including juvenile law, misdemeanor law, appeals, post-conviction work, felonies, drug cases, and vehicular cases, to name a few. Simply because you are focusing on one area of law does not mean you are doing the same thing over and over. I have handled thousands of cases, but I continue to be presented with new challenges and issues. I know criminal defense attorneys that do nothing besides DUIs or only handle juvenile criminal matters. I like doing misdemeanor and felony work because I like the variety, but every lawyer is different.

Where to Get Money for Your Practice

If you are independently wealthy when starting your practice you will have an easy road. However, I figure close to zero people reading this book are independently wealthy, so you will have to figure out where to get money to start your practice. There are many ways to get money, but not all the options are good for new attorneys.

There are traditional lenders, like banks and credit unions. The problem with traditional lenders is that they are hesitant to lend to new businesses. When I was starting my practice in 2009 there was a recession going on so banks were even more hesitant to lend than they usually are. The advantage you have as a solo practitioner when asking a bank for money is that you are likely going to be asking for less money than bigger businesses, which makes the lender less nervous. If you are asking for a loan to start a restaurant or another type of business that requires a lot of inventory, you will need more money. To start a law practice your requirements will be a lot simpler. Don't forget, simple is good.

If you do want to borrow money from a traditional lender, consider taking out a loan in your own name versus in the business name. The bank may be more likely to lend money to a person rather than to a new business. Obviously your credit score will play a large part in deciding if the bank will lend to you and, if they do, at what interest rate. When considering banks, talk to different ones and find one that treats you well. When I was looking for a bank, some banks were dismissive and condescending which obviously meant I was not interested in them.

Another lending option is the Small Business Administration (SBA). More information can be found about the agency at their website, sba.gov. As the name implies, they are a federal government agency designed to lend money to new businesses. One advantage of the SBA over banks or credit unions is that they generally charge a lower interest rate. One downside to the SBA is that they will take a long time to approve or deny your loan. Remember, you are dealing with the federal government and things take a long time. If you are applying for an SBA loan, you need to know that the process will likely take months and you have to plan accordingly. Another aspect to consider with the SBA is that they will require a lot of paperwork, from long applications to business plans, which you will need to prepare.

One option that I would recommend to others is a business credit card. I knew that I would only need a couple thousand dollars to get me going. I also knew that banks would not be interested in lending that little money. A few different banks explained to me that when it comes to business loans, they are not very interested in small amounts. Because of all the paperwork that the bank must complete, it is not really in their interest to lend small amounts. I found a credit card that had a zero percent APR for the first year and a low APR after that. I was essentially getting an interest-free loan. With credit cards it is important to remember to be careful about ballooning APRs. Be wary, when you are swiping a piece of plastic it often doesn't feel like you are spending real money, and it is easy to let the balance pile up.

When looking for money, don't forget about your family. If your parents or other relatives have a little bit of money to lend you at no interest or low interest this is not a bad idea. Family members will often be excited about investing in you and your business. Of course, there are also downsides when borrowing from family. First, if you lose money and become unable to reimburse your family, it can be embarrassing and put a strain on your relationships. Another possible downside is that your family may keep reminding you of how you needed their help to get started. I never considered borrowing money from my relatives, because it was important to me to do everything on my own. However, there is nothing wrong with going to family for help.

The last place I would consider looking for money is a special interest lender. If you belong to a religious group, ethnic group, minority group, or club you should do some research to see if they offer interest-free or low-interest loans. These types of loans often require a co-signer, so you may have to find someone who trusts you enough to co-sign. For example, in Phoenix there is an organization called Jewish Free Loans that gives interest-free loans to Jewish people starting a business. If you can qualify for an interest-free loan, you will be better off than if you have to worry about paying interest for years.

How Much Money Should You Have Before Starting?

There is no simple answer. One size does not fit all. The amount of money you need depends on the type of practice that you want to have. The location of the practice will also dictate how much money you will need before starting. A practice in Manhattan will require more money than a practice in a small town. If you plan on having associates and/or a staff, you will need more money. Also, you need to consider if you are going to work from home or have an office. Will it be an inexpensive office or a luxurious office? While there is no simple answer, below are some guidelines to keep in mind.

You must to have enough money to afford the essentials, like keeping lights on and the doors open. Some people will tell you need a year's worth of operating capital (how much money you need to keep the lights on and the doors open). Other people will tell you six months, while others will say three. My philosophy is that the more money you save up, the better, but you should have at least enough money to keep the doors open for a couple of months. You should figure that when you first begin your practice you will have very few clients.

In order to estimate how much capital you will need to start your practice, you should add up how much it will cost to run your business for one month and then multiply that amount by the number of months you can survive without making a profit. For example, if your monthly operating budget is one thousand dollars and you want to have enough for three months, you should have three thousand dollars saved up. If you encounter an expense that you pay annually, like bar dues, you can divide the total by twelve to get an idea of how much the expense is per month. If bar dues are $350 a year, the monthly cost is about $29.

Remember, in the real world you always end up spending more than you expect. This is just the reality of running a business. There will always be unexpected expenses. When I started my own practice, I ended up paying hidden fees to my credit card processing company. In this process, you should consider the following expenses:

- Office expenses (home office or traditional office)
  - Furniture
  - Rent
  - Fixtures
  - Kitchen supplies
- Taxes
  - State
  - Federal
  - Other
- Utilities (in particularly cold or really hot places, utilities can be incredibly expensive)
- Internet and phone costs
  - Business line
  - Cell phone
  - Messaging service
  - Monthly phone costs
- Postage
- Stationary
  - Business cards
  - Letterhead
  - Envelopes
  - Greeting cards
- Supplies
  - Paper
  - Pens
  - Notebooks
  - File supplies
- Support staff
  - Salaries
  - Worker's compensation
  - Retirement
  - Bonuses
  - Insurance

- Office Expenses
  - Software for client managing and finance management
  - Legal service subscriptions, such as Westlaw
  - Printers and paper
  - Files
  - Snacks and coffee
  - FedEx or process server costs
  - Parking costs
  - Computers
  - File backup programs
- Miscellaneous
- Bar dues
- Insurance
  - Malpractice insurance
  - Health insurance
  - Disability insurance
- Lunches
- Coffee
- Entertainment
- Money for clothing
- Dry cleaning
- Car
  - Gas
  - Car payments
  - Parking
  - Car registration
  - Maintenance and upkeep
- Living expenses
  - Rent/mortgage
  - Utilities
  - Cable and internet
  - HOA dues
  - Food
  - Entertainment
  - Travel

I include living expenses as part of your business because you not only have to keep your practice lights on, you also have to keep your home lights on. If you have a family and have a significant other that is working, this will help with your living expenses. When I started my practice, my wife was working, which covered a lot of our living expenses. Obviously some of you will not have a working significant other, so you will need to budget for all of your business expenses and personal expenses.

The above list is by no means exhaustive, but more of a starting point for costs to consider when deciding how much money you will need. Your costs will vary, depending on many factors. Some of your variables will be: Is your car paid off, or are you still making payments? Are you going to have a virtual office, a traditional office, or work from home? Can you find inexpensive used furniture, or are you going to spend thousands on new furniture? When I started my practice, my monthly operating budget was about $400 a month. I had almost no savings but I had my zero interest credit cards that I knew would keep me afloat for at least six months. A good general rule is to borrow as little as you can. Always remember that every dollar you borrow you will have to pay back, usually with interest.

Solo or Partner?

There are several advantages to having a partner. First, you are not going at it alone. You have someone on the same journey as you. When you have a partner there is always someone there to bounce ideas off of, to cover court appearances for you, and to help out in general. There is also a psychological advantage to knowing that you are not facing the daunting task of starting a law practice on your own. Another great benefit of having a partner is cost sharing. Instead of paying for an entire office you are paying for half of an office. Instead of paying for a copier you are paying for half of a copier, and so on.

Although there are benefits to having a partner, I think there are more drawbacks. I never considered having a partner and am glad I was on my own. One of the biggest problems when you are starting out with a partner is that there is usually not enough work for one person, much less two people. Author and law office management guru Jay Foonberg once wisely said that two people could starve just as quickly as one. If there is not enough work for one person there will not be enough for two.

Another problem with partnerships is that they are a lot like a marriage, and we know that over half of marriages do not survive. I once had a civil attorney tell me that he spends more time with his law partner than he does with his wife. This makes it extremely important to work with someone who you get along with. He also told me he has fights with his law partner just like he has with his wife. If you and your partner have a falling out, consider how the business will be divided. Who will get the clients, the building, and so on?

I remember learning something in my Business Organizations class in law school that seems to be true. It is not a matter of if a partnership will fail, but when. I have seen a lot of practices fall apart because the partners could not get along and had different goals. Remember, when you are on your own and you want the practice to go in a different direction, there is no problem. When you have a partner, the two of you need to agree. The more people involved, the more opinions there are and more opportunity to disagree.

There are many reasons that partners can have a falling out. Commonly, one partner will want the practice to go in one direction and the other will want something completely different. I knew two attorneys that started a practice and broke up the partnership within the year. One of the attorneys wanted to do felony cases and conquer the world. The other partner wanted to do a lot of misdemeanor work, go on a lot of vacations, and spend little time in the office.

Difference in work ethic is another cause for disagreement between partners. If one partner is working seventy hours a week and the second partner is working thirty hours a week, with the money being divided 50/50, how long will that partnership last? If one partner has three kids and is constantly taking time off for school events and other activities, while the other partner has no kids and never misses work, what is the future of the business?

Regardless, I know many attorneys that have had productive long-term relationships with their legal partners. Many partners have found success by keeping the money and fees separate. I would recommend anyone thinking about having a partner to consider this option. Even if you have a partner to share expenses with, you can still keep the money separate. If you have an "eat what you kill" style of arrangement, then each person can still work as much or as little as they want, without it affecting the other partner.

Attorneys who have successful partnerships must talk about the vision they have for the practice. Talking to a prospective partner initially in order to find out if you are on the same page is much more preferable to starting a practice only to THEN realize you have different goals. Many things must be discussed in detail. Some points to consider talking about:

- How is the firm's money divided?
- Will there be separate bank accounts?
- What will be the focus of the firm?
- How much vacation will each partner get?
- How will fees be split?
- Who will pay for what?

- How many hours a week will each partner work?
- Who will handle what part of the practice?
- Who will pay the bills?
- Who will bring in the clients?
- Who will travel for distant court dates?
- Who will make management decisions?
- Who will handle personnel issues?
  - Who handles the hiring and firing?
  - Who will be in charge of employee discipline?
- Who will handle trials?
- Who does appeals?
- How long do the partners want to be in the partnership?
- How much advertising will there be?
  - Who decides on advertising costs and how the advertising is done?
- How big or small will the firm be?
  - What if one person wants to expand and the other one does not?

After talking about everything there must be a partnership agreement. Think of it as prenuptial agreement. No one gets married hoping to get divorced but it's a good idea to be prepared. The partnership agreement must include information like how the firm will be dissolved, if one partner wants to buy out the other partner, what the procedure is, and what partner is responsible for what. Many partnership agreements can be found online. The best idea, however, is to go to a business attorney and have him draft the agreement for you.

Additionally, after the agreement is drafted, have each partner take the agreement to their own attorney for review. You will spend a little money paying for an attorney to draft the partnership agreement, but you will potentially save yourself a lot of stress down the road. Make sure your partner is someone you know and trust. I have heard too many sad stories of partners stealing money from each other, being deceitful, and so on. You may be spending more time with your partner than with your spouse, so make sure it is someone you like, someone you can work with, and someone you trust. Remember, you are looking for someone that you can work with, but also see daily and spend a significant amount of time with. You are not looking for a friend, but someone you can build a business with.

Different Office Options

First, you will need to decide if you want an office, and if so, what type. A traditional office is not necessary for new attorneys, mainly because of the cost. Say you find a great deal on an office for $400. Actually, $400 a month for an actual office in most markets is not realistic, but it will work for our example. You may think $400 a month is easily affordable. The problem with this logic is when you are starting out, $400 is a lot. Even if you are able to pay for the office, you are still wasting money. In a year you are spending $4,800 that you don't have to be spending. Those funds could be going into your pocket or be reinvested into the practice.

The type of practice you have will also dictate if an office is necessary. If you have a criminal defense practice, meeting clients at the courthouse is not a problem. Before I had a physical office, I would often meet clients at the courthouse and no one ever seemed to mind. I think some clients even preferred this method, because for them it was the equivalent of meeting a surgeon in an operating room. If you have an estate-planning firm, you will have to meet with clients and probably need to have an office. A home office is also an option that we will discuss soon.

The type of client you are trying to attract will also dictate the need for an office. If your specialty is banking law, and most of your clients are corporate executives, you must have an office. You can't meet a CFO of a bank at a Starbucks and tell him or her you don't have an office. Certain clients expect certain offices, because an office is a reflection of the attorney. If you are trying to present an exclusive, elite image to tackle high-priced clients, your office must reflect that image.

Moreover, I encourage young attorneys to begin without an office because it simplifies your life in several ways. Think of all the bills you won't have to worry about every month, as well as all of the headaches that go along with keeping up an office. Those of you who own houses know that something is always breaking and needing repair, and an office is no different. Offices have maintenance issues, such as electrical, heating, technology, and plumbing problems. Not having an office can also save time and money on commuting. If you are able to work from home, think of the time you can save by staying home instead of driving to your office. If you are located in large city with heavy traffic, not commuting can be a big advantage.

Some attorneys are worried about not having a traditional office because they fear that a client will think less of them if clients find out they don't have a real, physical office. I recommend that attorneys tell clients that you are saving them money by not having an office. Working from home or having a virtual office allows you to charge the client less, because your overhead is less.

Secondly, young attorneys must understand that most clients don't care if you have an office. Clients understand that current attorneys are more mobile than ever, and that an entire practice can be run from a smartphone. Do not be embarrassed if you choose to forgo an office. Turn a negative into a positive and explain to the client how they benefit from you being without an office. If you decide you need an office, there are several options.

The Traditional Office

The most traditional office option is paying someone to rent office space. The office can be in a small building with only a couple of spaces, or a large high-rise with hundreds of offices. The rooms themselves can range from under a hundred feet to many thousand feet. If you decide on a traditional office you need to discover how much space you require. The less space you need, the less money you will have to spend. Many places charge by square footage, so more space means more money. A perfect office should have enough space to make you comfortable, but not so much that it causes you to waste money or it makes the office feels empty.

These offices can come furnished or unfurnished. A furnished office will cost more, but will typically save time because you will not have to purchase furniture. If you have an unfurnished office and need furniture, consider buying used. Used furniture will cost much less than new furniture, and when you are starting fresh, every penny counts. If you have extra furniture at home or know of someone interested in donating office equipment, consider this option instead of buying new or used.

When you start looking for an office, you must do research. The process is similar to renting an apartment or a house — you need to check the place out. Some things to consider when choosing an office:

- How close is the office to your home?
- How is parking?
- How close is the office to the courthouse you use most?
- How safe is the neighborhood?
- Will clients like the neighborhood?
- Will clients like the building?
- How clean is the office?
- How long is the lease?
- What utilities are included?
- What time in the evening does the heat or AC get turned off?
- How often does the office get cleaned?
- Is there a kitchen or kitchenette?

Another good idea when visiting an office building is to talk to some of the other tenants. If the building manager is reputable, they will be glad to give you contact information for past and current tenants. If the building manager does not want you speaking to other renters, this is a red flag and you should walk away. By questioning other tenants, you will get a good feel for the building. Ask the current tenants if they enjoy working with the building management, if they like the space, and what (if any) complaints they have. The more information you acquire, the better-informed decision you will be able to make.

It is important to know from whom you are renting, especially if you are subletting. I almost learned this lesson the hard way. When I was starting out I met an attorney who seemed really friendly. She had an office to sublet and told me the office was one thousand dollars per month. I learned that one thousand dollars for that office was a terrible price, but she made it seem like a great deal.

I had a bad feeling about the whole arrangement and ended up walking away. The attorney tried to convince me by explaining how the office would practically pay for itself, and how I would generate a large profit by having the office. After I walked away I realized that the attorney had a terrible reputation and many people had problems with her. If I had gone through with the arrangement I am pretty sure the rent would have put me out of business and my firm would not have survived.

The point is that if you do get an office, do all of your research and be sure you know what you are getting yourself into. If you don't have all of the necessary information, walk away. Think of the movies that have the cliché where the star gets a bad feeling and doesn't commit the crime because he realizes it's a setup and the cops are waiting. Unfortunately, some landlords and other attorneys will take advantage of young, inexperienced attorneys.

Working from Home

Today, more and more attorneys choose to work from home. In the past, there was a stigma against attorneys working from home. The widespread belief was that a "real" lawyer needed an office. Many of those attitudes are shifting as technology and society advances. I know more than a few successful attorneys that have a home office with no interest in getting a traditional office. There are several advantages to working from home. One of the biggest is saving money on an office. You save money on not paying for a separate office space, but also on taxes. A home office can be a deduction that any knowledgeable accountant can tell you about.

A home office can also be a good way to save time. You won't need to drive to and from the office, thus eliminating a commute. Another benefit is that if you have kids, it can be a lot easier to monitor the children while working at home. One aspect to think about is the genre of your clients, and if you are willing to allow them into your home. I have a criminal defense practice, so a client coming to my house is out of the question. If you have an estate planning practice, however, you may agree to clients knowing where you live and visiting your home.

Also, simply because your office is located in your home does not mean that you are required to invite them in. Many attorneys will use a friend's office, or meet clients at coffee shops or restaurants. A lot of documents can now be shared via the Internet, so less face-to-face meetings are required than in the past. Something else to consider with a home office is that if you are having clients come to the house, will your homeowners insurance protect you? A good idea is to check your homeowners insurance to see what is protected. For example, if a client injures himself in your home, will you be covered?

One other factor worth checking is if the local zoning laws permit you to run a business out of your home. Zoning laws or local HOA rules may not allow you to have clients come to your house. A more efficient method is to check the local laws before starting your office at home, rather than to set up the entire office and find out it is prohibited.

Virtual Office

There are several variations of a virtual office. One option provides a service that answers your phone calls and takes messages. Some services forward your calls to a cell phone or a landline (if anyone still has a landline). Other virtual offices have meeting spaces or day offices that can be rented. Virtual offices can be a good option for attorneys who want the appearance of an actual office without having to pay for one. Some attorneys like virtual offices as a second location if they are trying to expand their practice with a second office. As more attorneys realize traditional offices are unnecessary, virtual offices are becoming more popular. Most major cities will have no shortages of virtual offices. They vary in price and location just as traditional offices do. Again, you must do your research and know what you are looking for.

When I started my practice I had a virtual office and it suited me well. I found an office building close to my house that offered virtual office services. For about 200 dollars a month, the office would sign for my mail, forward my calls to my cell, and if I didn't answer they would take a message for me. When someone called my office, an actual person would answer the phone and the computer would tell him the client was calling for me, so he would answer the phone as if he was my own receptionist. I enjoyed that it appeared as if I had my own receptionist while I was paying a fraction of the cost.

Another great service that my office offered was that they had conference rooms and day offices that I could rent by the hour. If I ever wanted to meet a client in the office or the conference room I would just reserve a space, and then when a client came in I would meet him or her in the conference room. As with everything there are some drawbacks to virtual offices.

Some virtual offices are very expensive and in my opinion not worth the cost. Another issue with virtual offices is they are not real offices, so if you want to use an actual office without paying by the hour you are out of luck. Something else to watch out for with virtual offices is the length of the contract. Many virtual offices will want you to sign long-term contracts. If the office is satisfactory, a long-term contract may be acceptable, but unfortunately you may not discover problems until you have signed the contract, and by then it is too late. Some things to consider when looking for a virtual office:

- Length of contract?
- Do other customers of the virtual office like the place?
- What is the penalty for violating the lease?
- Does the location have an actual physical office that can be used?
- Parking? (Covered parking?)
- Internet? (How fast is the Internet?)
- Printing services?
- Is everything one price or are there extra charges for phone answering?
- What hours will the phone be answered?
- Where do after-hour phone calls go?
- Will a local receptionist be answering your calls or will they go to a call center overseas?
- How late in the evening does the A/C or heat work?
- Location of the virtual office?
- Are there any hidden costs?

Overall, I think a virtual office can be a great option for a new law practice. When you are starting out, controlling costs is probably the biggest factor that will determine if your practice succeeds or fails. A virtual office can help control costs while giving the appearance of an actual office.

Office Sharing

There are a variety of office-sharing arrangements. The two most common are where the attorney subletting the office pays rent to the attorneys who own the office, or the new attorney does some work in exchange for the office space. One of the biggest advantages to an office-sharing arrangement is that other attorneys are around to offer mentorship and answer questions. Another advantage is the aspect of cost sharing. Instead of paying for everything on your own, the cost is divided between all of the attorneys. For example, if there are three attorneys, the costs are split three ways.

When I gave up my virtual office after having it for about eighteen months, I moved in with two attorneys that both practiced criminal defense work. Our arrangement was that they would not charge me rent, and in return I would make some court appearances on their behalf. It was beneficial for both of us, because they had an extra empty office and would be getting some free work out of me, while I got a rent-free office and more importantly would have two resources to go to with questions. I have been at the office for close to three years now and our arrangement still works well for everyone.

Something to keep in mind with office-sharing arrangements is that clients must understand that you have your own practice and are not in a firm with the other attorneys. An office-sharing arrangement can be confusing for clients because there are several attorneys in an office, which can look like a firm. The client must clearly know that they are hiring you, and only you, not the other attorneys in the office. A good idea is to have a line or two in your fee agreement that states you are not associated with the other attorneys in the office and only you will be working on the client's case. While considering office-sharing arrangements there are some things to think about:

- What is included in the arrangement?
  - Receptionist service, and if there is a receptionist, how will the phone be answered?
  - Postage?
  - Parking?
  - Utilities?
  - Who pays for office expenses?
    - Printer
    - Phone
    - Computer
    - Fax
    - Internet
    - Heat or A/C
  - Who pays for coffee/water services?
  - Cleaning services?
  - Who decides when the arrangement is terminated?

- Is there a written lease?
- If the office wants to buy something new how is the decision to purchase or not to purchase made?
- If the tenants want to move how will moving decisions be handled?

One last factor to consider is how well you know the attorneys you are sharing the office with. Before I began my office-sharing arrangement I asked my lawyer friends about the attorneys I was thinking of sharing an office with. I knew the attorneys in the office a little but I talked to a lot of people that knew them well. Only after I felt comfortable that the attorneys were reputable did I feel comfortable moving into their office. Like everything else, it is easier to do your research up front rather than have problems after you have moved in.

PO Box/Suite

One last aspect to take into account when choosing your office is to consider having a PO box. The biggest benefit of a PO box is cost. Most places will charge you about ten dollars a month for a PO box. Many attorneys that have home offices have a PO box for receiving services. The advantage to a PO box is that you can have a home office without giving your home address to clients. There is also the added benefit of having someone sign for your mail or packages in case you are not able to sign yourself.

Some mail services will provide you with a PO box for rent. They can also give you a box number, and those are called suites. The advantage is that your written address has "suite" instead of "PO Box" on it. One factor to be wary of with PO boxes is that many corporate commissions require a physical address and will not accept a PO Box. This can be a problem if you desire to form a corporation or an LLC.

Vision for Your Practice

When you start planning your practice it is important to envision the type of practice you want. Picking the type of law you want to practice is important, but a larger vision of your practice is also necessary. You must think about what type of clients you want to attract, how you plan on growing your practice, and if/when you hope to hire an assistant. Do you want an assistant and or associates?

The more questions you ask yourself, the better off you will be once you actually start your practice. I remember I spent over one year planning my practice. I spent time planning my office, where I wanted to live, and how I would pay for the practice. I thought about every possibility I could. I knew the more scenarios and possibilities for my practice I ran through in my head the better off I would be when I actually started my practice. Remember, the more you plan the better off you will be.

Legal Entity Formation

You must decide what type of entity your practice will be. Most small firms are either Limited Liability Companies ("LLC") or corporations. Every state has something equivalent to a corporation commission that will have all the forms available on their website. You want to make sure that you form some type of structure, whether it is an LLC or a corporation, to protect yourself. If you do not have an LLC or a corporation, you could be held personally liable in the case of a lawsuit or a judgment. Running your practice through an LLC or corporation can protect you.

Like with everything else, if you are not comfortable doing your own paperwork, you can hire an attorney to prepare the documents for you. Another advantage of going to a lawyer who specializes in this type of law is that they can advise you on what type of structure is best for your practice and why. One practice could be better off as an LLC while another could benefit from being a corporation.

The first time I applied for an LLC I checked a wrong box and had all the documents sent back to me, which delayed the entire process by several weeks. Most of the forms are not super complex and I would venture to say that if you can make it through law school and the bar exam you could figure out these forms. Remember, anything I can do you can probably do better.

Once you submit the paperwork, you need to publish the news of the formation of your company. Do your research when looking for a place to publish because the difference in cost can be noticeable. I found one newspaper that charged twice as much as a different newspaper. Once the articles are published the publisher will mail you a copy and will often mail notice of the publishing to the Corporation Commission. Don't assume the notice was sent the Commission and actually check to see if it was done.

Letting People Know You Exist

I see new solo attorneys make many different mistakes but one of the most common is not letting people know you exist. If the people around you don't know that you have a practice and are looking for cases how can they hire you? Everyone in your social and professional circle should know the following three things about you: (1) that you are a lawyer, (2) that you own your own practice, and (3) what type of law you practice.

Someone simply knowing you own a practice is not enough. Say you know someone that is looking for a divorce lawyer. If that person only knows you have a practice but doesn't know you handle divorce matters they may never come to you. Remember that people want to hire people that they know. Almost anyone would rather hire someone they know and trust rather than a stranger.

Ask yourself what groups, clubs, organizations, and social circles you belong to. Next, ask yourself if all the people in those circles know about your practice. If they don't you have work to do. There is also a ripple effect to letting people know about your practice. Your bowling league may only have ten people in it, but those people each know ten people and so on.

As discussed, getting clients is a numbers game. If ten people know you are a lawyer, you may get one person as a client. If 1,000 people know about you, you could get 100 clients.

Don't be afraid to ask people in your social and professional circles to spread the word about you. If people like you they will want to help. When trying to grow your practice the more people that know about you the better. Don't be shy when asking people to get the word out about you. The survival of your practice could depend on it.

Chapter 7

How to Make Money

So you have decided to start your own practice. You have picked a perfect office location, now comes the hard part. How will you make money and keep the practice afloat? The traditional way law firms make a profit is by having private clients. When you are new, this presents a few problems. First, most clients don't want to be your guinea pig. When you are searching for a surgeon to perform your operation, would you want to be the surgeon's first patient?

A new client may feel more comfortable with a new attorney depending on the type of work you would be doing for them. If you are doing estate planning and someone asks you to create a simple will, they probably won't mind that you are new. However, if someone comes to you to set up three different trusts involving foundations and charities, they probably won't be thrilled to hire someone new. Luckily, clients often do not ask how many cases you have handled. When I was doing my first jury trial, my biggest fear was that the client would ask if I had ever done this before. Thankfully, she never asked that.

The second problem for new attorneys when it comes to attracting clients is that it takes time to build up a client list. Most attorneys will tell you that it takes anywhere from five to ten years of experience before you gain a steady flow of private clients. Once you start getting clients, they come back to you and often refer friends and family, but the process takes time. This is not to say it's impossible to get a large amount of private clients immediately, but it's not typical. While your practice is forming, how does one generate enough money to survive?

Covering for Other Attorneys

One of the best ways for new attorneys to make money is unknown by young lawyers. When I started, I knew nothing of this method and had to have it explained to me, as I had no idea what it was. One of my main mentors told me I should "cover" for other attorneys. Covering for an attorney occurs when a lawyer is unable attend a hearing or appear in court, so you go in his place. An attorney may need coverage for a pretrial conference, a settlement conference, a trial, or any other type of courtroom setting.

An attorney may need an appearance covered for many different reasons. Like the aforementioned explanations, the attorney may be sick, out of town, have a scheduling conflict, forget about a court date, or simply not want to go. I once covered for an attorney that didn't want to reschedule his squash game. There are great benefits for covering for other attorneys.

The first is that you will make money. A coverage attorney will either charge by the hour or have a flat fee per appearance or day. When deciding how much to charge, discuss the local market with other attorneys. The market you are in will dictate what you can charge and what clients will pay. The wages are almost always less than what you would make from a private client, but when you are starting out, private clients will be limited and few and far between.

The second benefit is that you are constantly learning while you are working. When I began covering, I met judges and prosecutors that I practice with and in front of regularly. When you cover you begin to build your reputation. If you are professional, courteous, prompt, and ethical people will notice. Other attorneys and judges were aware I was new, but they saw that I was trying and hustling, which they respected. You not only get to go to court, but you get paid to go! Many coverage appearances are very simple and require easy tasks, like filing a motion to continue. Sometimes, however, coverage appearances can be complicated and involve cooperating with difficult clients, difficult prosecutors, or difficult judges.

Another benefit of providing coverage is the networking opportunities. You will likely cover for both good and bad attorneys. When you cover for skillful attorneys, you learn the correct way to run a law practice. You learn how to communicate with clients and how to practice properly. When you cover for bad attorneys, you learn what not to do. When I started covering, I didn't know very much about running a practice, so I learned a great deal from both types of attorney.

Coverage opportunities are never advertised, so everything is done by referral and word of mouth. I went from covering for one attorney to covering for well over 100 attorneys in a few years, all by reputation. Attorneys are like clients, if you perform well, they will tell other attorneys, who will in turn hire you. In the legal profession you have to have connections. You have to know people and people have to know you. Connections and relationships are not made overnight and must be built over time.

Elements to consider when covering for attorneys are plentiful. Some attorneys will intentionally throw you on figurative land mines. They may do it accidently or on purpose. Some attorneys will send you in their place if they know that the judge is mad at them or if there is a problem with the case. Some attorneys will not pay on time, so try to avoid covering for these attorneys as well. When you come across these attorneys, you should avoid covering for them in the future.

I once had to chase an attorney for close to a year to collect fifty dollars. I had covered a pre-trial conference for her and promptly sent her a bill. I will usually give a follow up phone call if an attorney has not paid in about a month. I called her and received no answer, so I left a voicemail. About a month after, I resent the invoice and tried to call again. Almost a year went by with no response from her. I ran into her almost a year later, and kindly informed her that she still owed me money. She did not apologize and wrote me a check. I never covered for her again.

Additionally, the type of law you practice may potentially limit your coverage opportunities. If you practice bankruptcy, family, or criminal law, opportunities to cover will present themselves, because court appearances are plentiful. If your area of practice provides few court appearances, you will see fewer opportunities. Keep in mind; you can fill in for more than just court appearances. You can cover depositions, interviews, and anything else where an attorney is needed.

Related to coverage, doing legal research for other attorneys is another way to network and earn money. Before I started covering, I did legal research for a number of attorneys. Lawyers like to hire people to do their research for them, because attorneys do not like to do their own research. Many attorneys believe that their time is too valuable to be doing research, and that their time can be better spent doing something else. Research can be tedious, but it is one method of getting money.

In order to find attorneys who need help researching, you need to know attorneys who are aware that you are available. When you meet an attorney, let him know that you are available for his legal research needs. If you don't inform people of your availability, they will never know.

Contracts

Almost every city and county will have various contracts available for attorneys. These positions vary, but generally they involve a county or city paying an attorney directly to handle cases. Cities and counties provide contract positions for many reasons. They can be civil or criminal and are an excellent way for attorneys to supplement their income. Contracts can offer more than a little extra income. A number of attorneys make a comfortable living doing just contract work.

Many types of contracts are prevalent in both cities and counties. In criminal practice, there are county, city, and federal contracts. At the federal and county level there are public defender offices but those offices are often conflicted off cases. There are many ways for an office to be conflicted off a case. One of the most common is if the office has represented a present co-defendant in a previous matter. If an agency is conflicted off a case private attorneys are brought in and paid directly by the government.

Private attorneys will also be brought in on occasion if there are not enough attorneys at an agency to handle the caseload. Contract work generally does not pay as well as private work, but often the work is steady and pays better than no work at all. Most cities, including Phoenix, do not have a traditional public defender's office employing full time attorneys. The city of Phoenix, like most cities in Arizona, pays private attorneys to handle criminal matters for indigent clients. Contracts are also available for juvenile and guardian work. Many cities will also have civil contracts for civil attorneys. For example, a city may have a contract reviewing proposed contract bids that the city is seeking. Just like criminal contracts, the pay will vary from contract to contract and city to city.

Contracts are often not advertised, but if they are, they are difficult to locate. An advertisement might be buried in some city or county website where no one will ever see it. Like many things in the legal profession, you must have connections that will inform you of when an opening appears. The best way to find out which contracts are available is to talk to an experienced attorney in your area. Some of the contracts require years of experience while others do not.

In general, the people in charge of the contract want to know whom they are hiring, so it is beneficial to know the people in charge. A good way to network is to spend time in the court where you are hoping to get a contract. Some cities have agencies that appoint the contracts. In some jurisdictions (mostly small towns) the judge assigns his own cases to local attorneys.

As the economy gets worse, more attorneys become interested in contract positions, because they provide job security. When jobs become more difficult to find, competition becomes more common. Currently, I have a contract with the City of Phoenix and there are always many more applicants than openings. A contract position can be a great way for young attorneys to learn, because of the variety the arrangement offers.

Family as Clients

When you are looking for work, don't forget about your family. If you are practicing in the same city as your family, go to them and ask them if they have any legal needs. I have an attorney friend who has a lot of family members that get arrested, and they always call him for help. Ask them if you can do a simple will for them for a few hundred dollars. You don't have to be an estate-planning attorney to figure out an uncomplicated will. Remember, your family is more likely to trust you when you are new. Often, family will ask you to provide free legal services, and it is your choice. On one hand, they will appreciate your work, but on the other hand, you are not making any money and your family may think you will always provide services free of charge.

Even if your family does not have any work for you, they may have friends that do. Make sure your family is telling people that you have a practice and that you can help with their legal matters. If you are doing estate planning and your parents have older friends, that is a potential source of clients. If you do criminal defense work and you have a brother whose friends are always getting arrested, that is also a potential source of clients.

Teaching

When you are starting out, consider teaching opportunities. Local community colleges, paralegal schools, and other institutions may be interested in having an attorney teach. Many teaching opportunities are not posted online and you have to know people that know people. As discussed earlier, networking is key. I got my first teaching job as a lawyer from a friend of a friend whom I used to cycle with. Another place to consider is an LSAT or bar prep center. If you received a high score on the bar or the LSAT, companies will probably be interested in hiring you to teach.

Today, there are more online schools and many of the schools are always looking for teachers. Teaching an online class can have the benefit of keeping your schedule free to do other work. Also, often the online teaching positions are easier to get than traditional teaching jobs. I know many experienced defense attorneys that teach online classes to supplement their income.

Lastly, consider tutoring opportunities for either high school or college students. The tutoring pay may not be wonderful but it will be a whole lot better than sitting at home making zero dollars. Ads for such positions may be posted in community blogs or local magazines and newspapers. Be creative where you look. Teaching may not be something you are passionate about, but work is work.

Seminars

There are many different types of seminars and many different ways to monetize them. A seminar is just a fancy word for a people listening to someone talk. Don't let the word seminar scare you. Your seminar doesn't need to have hundreds of people attending. A successful seminar could consist of five or ten people. I recently spoke to a lawyer that puts on seminars that teaches other lawyers how to get more clients and to streamline their law offices. The lawyer puts on one or two seminars a year and keeps the attendance to about ten to fifteen lawyers. The catch is that each lawyer attending pays about two thousand dollars to attend. The lawyer putting on the seminars has very low overhead as he doesn't have to rent a huge space and makes good money for a day's work.

Also remember to consider seminars for lawyers and non-lawyers, two very different audience groups that can benefit you in their own ways. These ways will be discussed later on in this section.

The most traditional seminar model is getting someone to pay to hear someone speak. There is nothing wrong with this model, but it will probably not work for new attorneys if they want to speak about an aspect of law. If you are a new attorney, chances are you will not have the wealth of experience in your area of law to get people to pay to listen to you speak. How many people are likely to pay for the following seminar:

COME LISTEN TO ATTORNEY WITH SIX MONTHS'
EXPERIENCE TALK ABOUT HOW TO TRY
A PERSONAL INJURY CASE

I'm going to go out on a limb and say that seminar will have low attendance (and by low, I mean likely zero people). There is a reason most lawyer seminars are conducted by lawyers with ten plus years of experience. I started this section by saying that a new lawyer will have a hard time putting on a seminar on substantive law. But, what about a seminar on something besides substantive law?

While no one may be interested in a new attorney talk about substantive law they may be interested in hearing the same lawyer present on something else. Say you have a background or interest in technology. Why not have a seminar, for example, on how to use PDF files to increase profits. In this hypothetical seminar, people thinking about going won't care how little legal experience you have, they will only care if you are an expert in PDFs.

This brings us to the next area that must be considered when considering putting on a seminar. Why should anyone care what you have to say? If you can't answer this question you are not ready to put on a seminar. You have to have something to offer or no one will want to attend your seminar. There are many examples of why someone might care about your seminar:

- You have a wealth of expertise in something;
- You have published a book or article and people are interested in your work;
- You have a new approach to an old issue;
- You have developed some kind of system that might help someone; or
- You have a high profile case that people are interested in.

The above list shows just a few examples. Use your own creativity to come up with reasons why someone may want to come hear you speak. So far we have been talking about putting on seminars for profit where the benefit to you is direct. You put on a seminar where ten people show up and pay you and you have made money. But what about seminars where the profit is not so direct?

Putting on seminars for potential clients is nothing new but I am always amazed how many attorneys don't take advantage of the idea. Say you are a new attorney trying to grow your estate planning practice. Why not put on a seminar in a nursing home? The topic could be anything that may interest elderly people and that will make them want to attend. While you don't charge anything for the seminar you potentially get one or two people to hire you. The profit is not direct as you are not getting paid for the seminar itself but you are still making money off the seminar as you are getting new clients.

As with many things we have talked about creativity is key. Think of where your potential clients are and how you can reach them. Think of places where you may be able to give a seminar. Your seminar will only be successful as the amount of time and planning you put into it. If you don't spend any time planning, promoting or advertising your seminar you can't be shocked when no one shows up.

Writing

I put the writing section right after the speaking section because the two can often complement each other. The more you write the more speaking opportunities you will have. The opposite is also true. The more you speak the more writing opportunities you will have. Say a person hears you speak at a conference and is impressed by your presentation. That person may ask you to write something for their magazine or website.

There are several ways that writing can help your practice. The first potential benefit of writing is that it can help you get more business. The more you write the more your name will appear online. When someone is Googling how to handle a divorce, and an article that you wrote pops up in the search results the person searching may hire you for the case. Remember that you will have heavy competition for clients. The great thing about getting clients through writing is that it is an easy way to reach out to potential clients. If you run a commercial or pay for Google AdWords, this will cost you money. Writing an article doesn't cost you anything and could still bring in new clients.

Another benefit of writing is that getting published helps to establish you as an expert among other lawyers. Being seen as an expert in a given area of law by other lawyers is incredibly valuable since those lawyers can refer business to you. Say you write an article for your bar journal on some aspect of construction law. A lawyer practicing criminal law reads your article and remembers that they have a client who needs someone who handles construction cases.

The last major benefit of writing is that you can make money off the writing directly. If your writing is good and you write things that are useful and interesting you can make money off your articles. Getting enough of a writing résumé for someone to pay you will take time but it is possible. Also, you won't grow rich from writing articles but when you are new and having a hard time paying your bills every dollar helps.

When thinking about writing don't just think of traditional articles. Think of new formats such as blogs. Remember that many potential clients don't care if your writing is in a magazine or online or on your own blog. If the content is good, relevant and informative people will read your work. Also don't forget about writing larger content like books.

Getting a book deal will not be easy but it is possible. I signed my first book contract with a major publisher after being in practice for less than four years. When people tell you it is impossible to get a book deal as a young lawyer don't listen to them. If you can't get a book deal, or don't want a book deal doesn't mean you can't write a book.

Today it is easier than ever to self-publish a book. Many publishing services won't even charge you a fee. Rather, the services will take a percentage of the book sale price. I have known several lawyers that have published their books for marketing purposes. The lawyers are not trying to sell the books (because they know no one will buy them) but want the books lying around the office.

When a potential client walks into their office and sees the book the lawyer is seen as more of an expert.

Other lawyers will offer to give away their book through their website if a potential client gives the lawyer their email. Getting a potential client's email is very important because then you can put them on your mailing list or newsletter. Even if they don't hire you right now they could hire you later on after being reminded about your services through a newsletter.

Building Up Private Clientele

The best way to make money in private practice is from private clients. Private clients will pay you more than court-appointed or contract-appointed defendants. The problem with building up a private client practice is that it takes time. Most attorneys build up a private client practice through referrals. The more happy clients you have, the more referrals you will get. Building up referrals takes time and new attorneys must remember to be patient.

Many experienced attorneys have told me that it takes anywhere from five to ten years to build up a private clientele. Obviously you may get lucky and start getting referrals earlier but, again, remember to be patient. One way to start building up a private clientele is by taking the clients that other attorneys may not want or may not have time for. Talk to attorneys you know and tell them that you would love their referrals. Other attorneys may give you their potential clients for several reasons.

The other attorney may be charging more than the client has. If the other attorney knows you are new and willing to do the case for less they can give you the referrals. The other attorney may also not want to deal with the client, as they are difficult and/or stubborn. They may have the luxury of turning away the difficult client, but you do not. When I started I had an attorney refer a case to me in northern Arizona because she did not want to make the drive. I was more than glad to make the drive and made some money in the process. The client in northern Arizona referred me to his roommate, so I got two clients out of one. If you do a good job for your clients, eventually the referrals will come and your private clientele will grow. I have been in private practice for four years and I am just now starting to build up a regular private client base. New attorneys must work on getting referrals but they must also work on keeping current clients.

Some clients will refer you to their friends and some clients will come back to you in later cases. In criminal defense work many clients get into trouble over and over. If they like their defense attorney they will go to them again.

For example I have had defense attorney friends that have represented the same defendant on three different DUIs. In civil cases, you may have a client that comes back to the same attorney for different lawsuits or other civil matters.

Importance of Having Different Streams of Income

As an attorney, you should always be careful that your income is never dependent on one source. A good attorney must diversify their sources of income. Anyone that has ever watched an investment show or read how-to books about Wall Street will have heard about the importance of diversification. In a stock market sense, the term means that an investor should have diversity in the types of stock they own. The logic is that if one sector of the economy slows down only a part of the investor's portfolio will be invested. If an investor does not have a diverse portfolio they could be wiped out. The same logic applies to attorneys.

If your entire income is dependent on one type of income, and that source of income goes away, you will be in serious trouble. If 100 percent of your income is one single contract, and you lose that contract your practice will have to close. No matter how profitable one source of income is you must remember that it can always go away. I have known many defense attorneys that were 100 percent dependent on private clients. For whatever reason, the private clients dried up. When the private clients dried up, the attorneys had no means of making money.

The more sources of income you have the more stable your practice will be. In my practice I have five separate sources of income: (1) one contract, (2) private clients, (3) coverage for other attorneys, and (4) being a law professor, and (5) being an author. I know that I could lose any one at any time. For any number of reasons one source of income could always be taken away. As long as I have other sources of income I will always be OK financially. For me, an attorney who only has one source of income is like rock climbing without a safety rope.

Should You Advertise?

There are different attitudes about whether new attorneys should advertise. One viewpoint is that new attorneys must advertise to get new clients. Some attorneys will tell you that even if you have to take out loans to pay for the ads, it is worth it. They will tell you it is worth it because the ads will bring in enough clients to pay for the ads plus you get your name out there.

In my opinion, as new attorneys, you should not advertise. The first reason has to do with cost. Advertising is incredibly expensive. In the Phoenix, Arizona, market in 2012, a fifteen-second television commercial cost about $300. That $300 is to run the advertisement once. Radio and print commercials cost less but are still very expensive. When you have a new practice you should be counting your pennies, and advertising is not the best use of your money.

The second reason I am not a big advocate of new attorneys advertising is because in order for the advertising to be effective, you must have a lot of ads. I learned this first hand when I ran an ad in the local college paper. The guy selling the ad promised me all kinds of things and the ad was for a 1/4 of a page and cost $200 dollars a week. The paper had a circulation of about 200,000 people. I figured if I gained one client out from the ad, it would pay off. After running the ad for six weeks I did not get a single client, a single call. Part of the reason is because no one reads newspapers. If someone does look at a paper, it is in passing.

Another part of the reason the ad produced no clients is because Phoenix has hundreds of criminal defense lawyers, many of whom spend small fortunes on advertising. Between TV, radio, billboards, bus ads, and other types of ads, the legal field does not have a shortage of attorneys. My print in the paper never had a chance against a firm spending tens of thousands and sometimes hundreds of thousands of dollars a month on ads. I am not opposed to advertising; I think if it is done correctly it can produce results. However, for the aforementioned reasons, I generally advise new attorneys to do little to no advertising.

If you are interested in advertising, consider guerrilla marketing/advertising. The term was coined by someone much smarter than me, and deals with getting free advertising. Consider contacting a local paper and ask them if you can write a column for them. Contact local TV channels and ask if they ever have some kind of an "Ask A Lawyer" segment that you could come on for.

Another good way to get your name out there for free is with online services that answer legal questions to the general public at no charge. Services like Avvo.com have attorneys that answer people's questions and people can hire an attorney that they find on the website. Avvo does an attorney rating for every attorney who is a member. One of the ways to increase your score is to answer people's legal questions. Answering questions is free and a good way to get your name out there. Avvo, like everyone else, will try to sell you a premium subscription but the base membership is free. Avvo is just one example and there are many websites like it.

Another good way to get free advertising is to make instructional videos for potential clients. Today, more and more people are using YouTube as a search engine. What this means is that if you can get a prospective client to watch your video they may hire you after watching your video. The videos don't need to be fancy or glossy. Think of the videos as video blogs. The videos don't need to be anything more than you sitting at a desk talking about some legal issue. Don't worry about buying a big expensive video camera and expensive video editing software. Today an iPhone can produce amazing video. As far as editing software there are many low cost editing tools available on line. As with other things we have discussed you can pay someone to edit your videos, but obviously this will not be free.

Try to make videos about areas of law that your potential clients are interested in. If you are a family law attorney, a video on environmental regulation will probably not get you many potential clients. As streaming video becomes a bigger and bigger part of our lives the lawyers that learn this technology will reap the most benefit. The videos can benefit your practice in two different ways. First, you can use the videos to drive traffic to your website from services such as YouTube. Second, you can post the videos directly on your website so that potential clients already on your website can watch the videos.

Be creative and think of ways to get advertising. You will have less money than established firms but you will have more creativity and time, which you should use to your advantage. If you think of some clever, free advertising and you try it and it produces no leads, you have not lost anything, because you didn't pay anything.

Chapter 8

Professionalism

Reputation is everything for a lawyer. This might be the single most important thing I can teach you. Let me say it again in all capital letters. REPUTATION IS EVERYTHING. A good reputation stays with you throughout your entire career. A bad reputation does the same thing. An attorney's reputation affects every part of their practice. How clients, prosecutors, opposing counsel, judges, court support staff and everyone else you work with view you is affected by your reputation.

Every day I work with attorneys with excellent reputations and with terrible reputations. The attorneys with excellent reputations get better offers from prosecutors, more extensions from judges, better dates from bailiffs and enjoy many other benefits. The attorneys with terrible reputations get the opposite. Another thing that's important to remember about reputations is that they are not stagnant. An attorney's reputation is always getting better or getting worse. There is also a snowball effect. If your reputation is getting better, it gets better quicker over time. The same thing is true about a bad reputation.

Young attorneys must remember that they are always being judged and evaluated. Every time you go to court, every time you file a motion, every time you talk with a prosecutor or opposing counsel you are being judged. The person dealing with you is deciding whether they think you are competent, professional, courteous and pleasant to work with or not. Part of establishing a positive reputation is always being mindful of your own possible arrogance.

I have seen many young, and some not so young attorneys have their reputation ruined by arrogance. There is nothing worse than when I see a young attorney be rude or arrogant to staff support person like a bailiff or a clerk, or anyone for that matter. This is close to professional suicide. Lawyers must remember to be humble and to not only not be arrogant, but to not even be perceived as arrogant. In the case of arrogance, perception becomes reality. Arrogance is not to be confused with confidence. A good attorney should be confident and carry him or herself in a confident manner.

A young attorney must remember that everyone in the legal community talks and most attorneys know each other. Not only do attorneys talk to each other but also they talk to bailiffs, clerks and judges, and all those people talk to each other. When a young attorney is arrogant to a bailiff in one court he or she often doesn't realize that the bailiff will not only talk to his judge, but to other bailiffs and other attorneys.

I am amazed at how often an interpreter, bailiff or prosecutor will tell me about what some other attorney did or what they heard about some other attorney doing. The lesson in this is that everyone talks. This can either be a benefit or a problem. If you do things right, people will talk about that. If you do things wrong and are arrogant, I can guarantee you people will talk about that.

I know one attorney who started his own practice and things were going well, but at some point he took a wrong turn and became arrogant. He started telling people about how well he was doing, and about how successful his practice was. He began to irritate people with his attitude and soon people began to talk. After a while his reputation was tarnished, and now it will be virtually impossible for him to undo that. I would recommend you learn from his experience and not make the same mistake yourself. As everyone knows, it's much easier to learn from other people's mistakes than your own.

Here is a quick story about how reputation works. My wife used to work at a firm and they had an associate that was wildly incompetent. He missed deadlines, screwed up cases, and was essentially a walking malpractice suit. My wife's firm did not handle criminal cases. One day I saw that young associate in criminal court. He had started his own practice and was now handling criminal matters.

He didn't know that I knew about him because he forgot how small the world is and how everyone knows everyone. Before he ever talked to me I knew he had a bad reputation and that reputation affected how I dealt with him and what I passed along about him to my lawyer friends.

Negotiating

Negotiating is a large part of what lawyers do. As a lawyer you will negotiate with opposing counsel, venders, clients, judges, and lots of other people. A lawyer hoping to run a successful practice must be a good negotiator. If you want to know how to negotiate correctly read *The Godfather* by Mario Puzzo. There are many great lessons for lawyers in the book, but the most valuable, in my opinion, is how to negotiate. When the Godfather negotiates he gets the best possible outcome and he does so because he follows simple rules.

The first rule is to never be emotional when negotiating. Generally, the person that sticks to logic and avoids emotions will get the best outcome. When someone is upset with the Godfather, he never loses his cool no matter how emotional the other person becomes. I often have to deal with a client who is either emotional or downright hysterical. If I become emotional in return this doesn't help anyone.

The second rule is to be fair. While you want the best outcome for yourself or your client when negotiating always remember that what you are asking for must be fair and reasonable. Often, lawyers get carried away and begin to ask for things that are unreasonable. Other times clients will push you as the lawyer to ask for something that is unreasonable. This happens to me often when a client wants me to ask for a plea agreement that is completely unreasonable. If a prosecutor offers a plea agreement for ten years in prison, then it would be unreasonable for me to ask for probation.

The third and final rule is to have all the facts when you come to the negotiating table. If you have not thought of all the possible angles and possible outcomes of a deal you are negotiating, then you have not done your job well. Always be as well informed as you can when negotiating. Sometimes you will have done everything you can and still not have all the facts, this is OK. Your job is to do the best job you can with all the information you can gather.

Punctuality and Calendaring

It seems easy and obvious that attorneys should be on time. Despite this, I am amazed how often attorneys show up late. The problem with showing up late is that it annoys people. Being late annoys clients, opposing counsel and, worst of all, judges. If you are running late, always call the court and tell them you are running late. Even if you are only a little late, the court will appreciate the gesture. I am not saying you cannot be thirty seconds or one minute late but if people have to wait for you they will remember it. Some judges are less forgiving about punctuality than others. I have seen more than a few attorneys get yelled at by judges for repeatedly being late. No one enjoys having an angry judge with a courtroom of people watching.

Obviously, things will come up and you will be late from time to time. Courts run late, traffic jams happen and unexpected things come up. As an attorney, part of being professional is to let the court know and to not make a habit of being late. Frequently, I will have two court settings in the same building at the same time. It is clear that I will not be able to be in the same place at the same time. When I go to court, I will go to the second courtroom and tell them I have to be in a different courtroom, and that I will come to the second courtroom as quickly as I can. I will usually also leave my cell phone number with the bailiff so the court can get a hold of me if they need to.

A big part of punctuality is calendaring. Calendaring is the simple practice of writing down dates in a paper or electronic calendar. It is impossible to be a good attorney without keeping a good calendar. There is no perfect way to calendar, but it is something that must be done. The practice is not difficult but one that must be learned early. When you are starting out you may be tempted to just remember dates in your head. This is a terrible idea and must be avoided. Always write down dates. You do not want to be standing in front of an angry judge explaining that you had the court date in your head but forgot.

A calendar is only useful if it is used regularly. Not only must you put all your appointments and court dates into it, you must also check it regularly. I usually check my calendar every evening to make sure I know where I am going in the morning and that I have not forgotten anything. It doesn't matter if you use a traditional paper calendar or an electronic one on your phone or computer, but you must have one.

One of the simplest and best calendar programs is Google Calendar. My favorite aspect of the program is that it automatically updates between devices. You can enter something from your phone and it will show up on your computer. There are much fancier and more expensive programs but I think they are usually not needed. Google Calendar is free, easy to use and easy to update. A word of caution about calendar software — calendar software, like all software and computers, sometimes break. I keep an electronic calendar but I also use a good old-fashioned paper calendar. I know the paper calendar will never shut off or delete all my appointments.

Going to Court

In virtually every office or court setting there are people that you want to see and people you don't. The people you don't want to see do nothing but complain. They are not fun to be around. Sometimes they are stressful to be around, and sometimes they are downright unpleasant. Every office and work place in the world has this type of person. People do not like them, and talk behind their back about how they do not like them. There is also another type of person in every office.

The second type of person is someone people like to be around. This person is positive, pleasant, polite and enjoyable to be around. This type of person makes small talk, asks people about their weekends and remembers people's hobbies. You get the picture. When you go to court you find the same two types of people. Your goal is to be the second type. Your life will be easier and people will do more for you when they like you. Don't be fake and pretend to care because people can tell. Be polite and friendly. Your goal should be when someone sees you coming they smile and look forward to talking to you.

When you go to court it is important to know your personality. If you are quiet and shy there is nothing wrong with this. If you are shy and introverted don't try to be outgoing and boisterous. If you are naturally outgoing and love to talk to people don't try to be withdrawn. No matter your personality always be polite, friendly and the type of person people like to be around. How you behave is obviously important. How you dress is also important.

When you go to court you must dress like a professional. This seems as obvious as the fact that you should be on time, but I am always amazed at what I see attorneys wearing to court. When you are an experienced attorney, people will not judge you on your clothing because they know that you are either competent or you are not. When you are a new attorney, court personnel and clients do not know if you are competent. The only thing people in court know about you when you first show up is how you are dressed. If it is your first time in court and you are a female attorney and you show up in a low-cut shirt, in a short skirt and clear heels, what kind of image does that present? You may think I am making up the clear heels but I have seen a female attorney come to court in clear heels. You can't make this stuff up.

On more than one occasion I have brought female students to court and after the students left other attorneys made comments to me about how the students were not dressed appropriately. The attorneys that saw the students didn't know anything about the students but they knew how they were dressed. It is not fair that attorneys are judged on their clothing but it is a fact of life so you must plan accordingly. It is also not fair that female attorneys are judged more on their clothing than male attorneys but this is also a fact. I always tell my students to go out and to spend a little bit of money on nice clothing. When dressing for court here are some things to keep in mind:

- Are your shoes polished?
- Are you wearing anything that could be perceived as inappropriate?
- Are your shoes appropriate for court?
- Are you clean-shaven? (Do you look like you just woke up?)
- Are your pants properly hemmed? (Alterations are cheap, and worth it.)
- Do your clothes match?
- Are you wearing a lot of perfume/cologne?
- Is your outfit drawing attention to you? (Is it good attention?)

- Do you look like a professional?
- Does your belt match your shoes?
- Do you look like you would want your attorney to look?

A lot of your clothing will depend on what court you are in. For example, in Federal court men and women are expected to wear a jacket. In most of the city courts, a jacket is not required and many attorneys will not wear a jacket. When you are a young attorney and dressing for court, you should always err on the side of caution. It is always better to look too conservative than too outlandish. Keep in mind there is nothing wrong with having your own style as long as that style is appropriate for the court you are in.

When I began to practice several attorneys joked with me that I rarely wore a white dress shirt and tended to wear colored dress shirts. There is nothing wrong with colored dress shirts as they are still dress shirts and I always wore a tie. If I had showed up in a bright colored tank top that would have been a problem. You will have plenty of time to develop your own style so be careful about people judging you on your clothing.

Dealing with Others in Court

As already discussed your reputation is key. Reputation determines how judges view you, how much the prosecutors listen to you and how everyone treats you. When you are new, you don't have a reputation yet and you must constantly be careful to do the right things so that you can build a positive reputation and not a negative one.

Any experienced attorney will tell you that some of the most important people in the court are the bailiffs and clerks. The support people are not ruling on your motions, but make no mistake they are incredibly powerful in their own way. Bailiffs and clerks determine when your matter is set, when the judge hears your case, and a lot of other matters that can simplify your life or make it more difficult.

The difference between a bailiff liking an attorney or not liking them can mean the difference between the judge hearing your matter right away or in two weeks. A young attorney should be nice and courteous to the support staff simply because it is the right thing to do, but also because all the bailiffs and clerks talk. They not only talk to each other but they talk to their judges. You never want to be called into the judge's chambers and have the judge ask you why you think it's OK to be rude to his or her bailiff. Almost every week I see an attorney be rude or arrogant to a court support person and it always amazes me that they are so actively sabotaging their careers. In addition to dealing with support staff, you will spend a lot of time dealing with prosecutors and opposing counsel.

Some attorneys think that if they yell and throw papers at the prosecutor or opposing counsel this will be beneficial to their clients. I think some attorneys do it to put on a show for their clients. Some clients believe that if their attorney is being "aggressive," they are fighting hard for them. What always amazed me about this is that, as a defense attorney, I am always trying to get something from the prosecutor. The prosecutor is the one that makes the offer to my client. If I am trying to get a better offer from a prosecutor, why would the prosecutor make me a better offer when I am yelling at them?

Prosecutors are people and they remember how attorneys treat them. I know that I can go up to any prosecutor that I have ever worked with and if I ask them for something they will at least consider it. They also know that if I am asking them something it will be for something reasonable. It is amazing how many defense attorneys I see being rude or condescending to prosecutors. There are several problems with this. The first problem is that we work with the same prosecutors a lot. Depending on the court, I may have close to a hundred cases a year with the same prosecutor. The second problem is when you are rude to prosecutors this affects your reputation. Don't forget, reputation is everything.

The last person worth mentioning is the judge. They are easy to find as they usually have a black robe. There are a few simple rules for appearing before judges. Even if you do not like the judge personally, you must show respect to the court. Always stand when speaking to the judge. It is not improper to speak to judge while sitting, but it is another way to show respect to the court. Never talk over the judge. When the judge is talking you are not. Lastly, get to know your judge. Every judge has his or her own quirks. Some get furious if you chew gum, others get mad if you are one minute late. Other judges do not want you walking around the courtroom during trial. Always remember that it is THEIR courtroom and that they make the rules — simple rules, but ones many attorneys forget. There is one judge that holds my hand when talking to me. Do I think this is strange? Of course I do, but it's their courtroom, their rules.

Ethics

Entire law school classes and many books are devoted to professional responsibility and ethics for lawyers. My goal here is to briefly give pointers to help young attorneys avoid ethical pitfalls. As a young attorney there will be many ethics hazards that you will have to negotiate. Young attorneys have to deal with issues ranging from how to handle money to client issues, from rules of court to rules of evidence.

One great resource available to young attorneys is talking to experienced attorneys. When I was new I would call other attorneys almost every day with a ton of questions. I would ask questions about all kinds of stuff such as how much to charge, how to handle a difficult client and many other questions. Remember that more experienced attorneys have most likely had the issue that you are now facing. Most experienced attorneys do not mind and actually like helping young attorneys. If one attorney doesn't know the answer to your question try a different one.

Another good resource that is available to most attorneys is an ethics hotline that is run by the state bar. In Arizona, attorneys at the state bar staff the ethics hotline and speak to attorneys and answer their questions. These attorneys are very knowledgeable and helpful. When I was new to practicing, I once had a prosecutor subpoena me to court because I had a client who wanted out of his plea. I was not sure how much I could tell the court about what the client had told me before he entered the plea so I called the hotline.

The hotline attorney was incredibly helpful and I felt a lot better after speaking to him. As a young attorney, you must always be careful to comply with the ethics rules in your state. The best way to do this is to actually know the rules. In Arizona, the rules are available online and can be easily accessed for reference. As you become more experienced the rules will become second nature but when you are new you will need to refer to them from time to time.

When I teach Professional Responsibility, I tell my students that on an exam if they do not remember the specific rule to pick the answer where the attorney is honest and discloses everything, and often that will be the correct answer. In practice the same idea is true. Always err on the side of being too honest. Being too honest will never get you into trouble like lying will.

This seems simple but many attorneys forget the importance of honesty. Just last week, I learned of an attorney that told his client not to come to court for a hearing. When the judge asked the defendant where his client was, the attorney lied. The attorney told the judge he did not know where the client was. The attorney ended up getting suspended from the practice of law when it was learned that he told his client not to show up.

There are a couple Model Rules that are worth discussing. Virtually every state has some version of the Model Rules. I am using the ABA model rule numbers. The specific numbering for your state may be different. There are a several rules that are worth discussing in some detail.

> Client-Lawyer Relationship Rule 1.1 Competence: A lawyer shall provide competent representation to a client. Competent representation requires the legal knowledge, skill, thoroughness and preparation reasonably necessary for the representation.

To a new attorney this rule may be scary because it is hard to know what you are competent to handle.

A new attorney must be reasonable with himself or herself as to what they can honestly handle. A new attorney should not be afraid to take on a new type of case and learn along the way. While it is good to handle a new type of case a new attorney must also not take on more than they can handle. If you are a criminal defense attorney and you do a lot of misdemeanor DUI work and you decide to take on a felony DUI even though it would be your first this is reasonable. If you are a DUI attorney and you decide to take on a murder case this would likely be a violation of rule 1.1. A new attorney must balance having enough work to pay the bills and to learn, and taking on work that you cannot handle.

Another set of rules that new attorneys must follow is the conflict rules. ABA Model Rules 1.6, 1.7, and 1.8 deal with conflicts. The rules should be read carefully and often. The rule of thumb is if you think there is a conflict or a possible conflict avoid the conflict. Some conflicts are obvious. Representing two sides that are litigating against each other is an obvious conflict. Some conflicts are not as obvious and attorneys must be careful.

ABA Model Rule 7.1 deals with advertising. New attorneys must know that they can advertise but must follow specific rules. For example, in Arizona an attorney's advertisement must feature several things. The ad must contain the name of at least one attorney in the firm, the firm's address and the name of the firm. There are no rules that ads must be classy or professional but a new attorney must always think of their reputation and how they will be perceived in the community. As a new attorney do you want to be thought of as the person with the tasteless, tacky ads?

Trial

A few quick words on trial. Often the attorney that is best prepared wins. A lot of people think trials are about showmanship and presentation. While those things can be important being prepared is by far the most important thing. Being prepared means several things. You must know the facts of your case inside and out. I have seen many prosecutors that do not know the facts of their case. In many cities, the prosecutor is assigned the morning of the trial. As you will know your case and have had it for several months this can give you an advantage. Being prepared also means you know the law. You know the statute, the positive case law, the negative law and how various cases can affect your case.

Another part of being prepared is having your client ready. You have to know what your client is going to say. You must not only know what the client is going to say but how they are going to say it. I once lost a jury trial because my defendant got on the stand and said the video that the jury just watched never happened. The client must also know what to expect. They must know what the opposing counsel or the prosecutor is going to say. How long the trial will take, and who the witnesses are.

You as the attorney must remember that the whole process is new and scary for the client and plan accordingly. Think of a surgeon before an operation. The surgeon has probably done the procedure hundreds if not thousands of times, but the patient is still scared and worried. The patient is worried and scared because they have never had the surgery. Clients are the same way. The more the client knows what to expect, the more at ease they will be and they less they will bug you. The less your client is bugging you the more you can focus on the trial.

Always remember to dress for trial. Be aware that you do not generally want to look flashy. Remember that the jury is evaluating how you are dressed and if they don't like how you look they can take that out on your client. I have a defense attorney friend who once had a juror tell him that she convicted his client because she did not like the attorney's shoes. This is not rational but jurors are people and you do not want to offend them. Always wear a jacket to trial. A lot of the time I will only wear a shirt and tie to court but I will always wear a jacket to trial. If the prosecutor is wearing a jacket and you are not the jury can think you are being disrespectful to the court.

The last important thing that new attorneys must remember is the value of brevity. What I mean by this is if you can say something in a few words, don't use a few hundred words. Often new attorneys think that the longer they talk, the better it is for their case. In reality, often the person that can make a short powerful statement is going to be better off. Juries and judges today have shorter attention spans than ever before. Attorneys must know this and prepare their arguments accordingly. Just as good writing should cut out everything that is not necessary, arguments in trial should do the same. Before trial, look at your written opening, cross, closing, and everything else and ask what you can cut out.

Interviewing and Résumés

I first realized how bad most law students and recent law school grads were at interviewing when I began doing mock interviews at a local law school. The program is designed to help students get better at interviewing. I was amazed at how many of the students were not prepared to give a good interview. It doesn't matter if you own your own practice or hope to work for someone else, you will have to go through interviews. I think since I have started my own practice, I have probably been through half a dozen interviews for various positions or contracts.

Interviewing, like everything else, takes practice and preparation. Some aspects of having a good interview are simple, and I don't need to spend a lot of time on them. You must be on time. This sounds simple, but I am always amazed when I see people coming in late to interviews. If you can't come on time to an interview, how will you come to work on time? If I am interviewing someone and they show up late, I know I will not hire them no matter how much I am impressed by them or how qualified they are.

Always remember that you must convince the person that is interviewing them how you will help them. Don't focus on how they can help you. Often I am at interviews where the person tells me that the job they are interviewing for would be a great opportunity and how excited they would be to work there. The person interviewing you doesn't care that they can help you. The person interviewing you cares how you can help them. Can you make their lives easier? Can you bring in clients? Can you show up on time and do good work? Always focus on what you bring to the table. You have to sell yourself. An employer wants to know that you are hard-working, motivated, and driven. As I have mentioned, I can teach someone to practice, but I can't teach someone to be motivated.

Another key aspect of interviewing is showing excitement for the work. Not the fake kind of excitement, but a real showing that you want to be working there. The person interviewing you can tell if you want the job or not. Also remember that you are likely not the only person being interviewed, and you must convince the employer why they should hire you and not someone else. Before you ever get to an interview, you must have a résumé.

Simply put, you must have a perfect résumé. Your résumé can't be good, very good or any other variation of good. Your résumé must be perfect. I have talked to countless employers that do not initially read résumés. They look at a résumé to see if they like the layout and how the résumé looks. If they do not like how the résumé looks, they simply throw it away. The information in your résumé could be amazing, but no one will read them if the résumé gets thrown away before being read. It is not uncommon for an employer to receive hundreds of résumés for one position. I know one government agency that recently received over 200 applications for one position. I also know of a local firm that was looking for a paralegal. That firm received over 400 résumés. Hopefully, you are beginning to understand why your résumé must be perfect.

There are several things you can do to make your résumé look better. Make sure that everything lines up. When you look at your résumé everything must be in place and neat. There are many examples of résumés online if you need samples. Your résumé should not be longer than one page. I have had many employers tell me that they do not like stapled résumés and will often not look at the second page. Many employers do not like résumés that are over one page because longer résumés create more volume.

If an employer has 400 résumés and each one is two pages, that's 800 pages of paper. Another reason your résumé should be one page is because you should be able to fit everything important on a single page. No one cares if you played volleyball in high school or what clubs you were in in middle school. Your résumé should start with college. Like everything you write and will be turning in to someone your résumé must be proofread. The more people that proofread your résumé the better. An employer will glance at your résumé for a split second and decide if they want to read it or not. If your résumé looks anything less than perfect, they will throw it away. Prepare accordingly.

Constant Improvement and Being Flexible

An attorney should always be working on improving their craft. It should not matter if you are in your first year of practice or your fiftieth you should always be trying to improve. The constant goal of improving is a characteristic that all excellent attorneys have. It doesn't matter if the area of improvement is trial skills, client management, organization or any other facet of practice. If you are not constantly working on getting better you will never grow. Think of an athlete or performer. How good would an athlete be if they were not constantly working on getting better? What if a sprinter said I'm pretty good now, but I don't want to get any faster?

A lot of always getting better at your craft has to do with mindset. If you have a mindset that says "I can get better at the following things," you will be more likely to improve. If you have a mindset that says "I know as much as I need to know and I don't need to learn anything new," this will hold you back. It is important to tell yourself that no matter how skilled you are at something you can always improve. Even if the improvement is small it is still an improvement.

Another important reason why you should always be trying to improve is that it will keep the work more interesting. If you are always doing the same thing and content to be at the level you are at you will get bored. One of the best things about the legal profession is that there is always room for growth. It doesn't matter what type of law you practice there is always something new to learn. There is always a new way to organize your office, a new way to do a trial opening, or a new way to reassure a nervous client. An important part of always improving is staying flexible.

A good attorney must be flexible in how they do things. If someone has a way of doing something that is better than how you do it why not adopt the new method? If you have always done jury closing one way but someone tells you about a method that is likely to be more effective why not try it? Often attorneys will be inflexible and not willing to try different approaches. Once I was talking to a prosecutor about how she was marking files. I told her that the way she was doing it was hard to read and confusing and suggested a different way that would be easier for her and for me. She told me that she had always done it the other way and would not change.

Today, after having thousands of clients, I still talk to other attorneys and ask for their advice and suggestions on how I can improve. Just last week I was at a party with an excellent defense attorney who suggested I change one part of how I talk to clients. Instead of being defensive and telling her that my method was fine I listened to her and thought about what she said. I realized that she was correct and I have since adopted her suggestion in how I speak to clients. As an attorney you will have people suggest things to you all the time. Not all the suggestions will be good but you should always keep an open mind to doing something differently.

No matter what type of law you practice you will have clients with mental health issues. Many people think it is only criminal defense clients with mental health issues but this is not true. Attorneys in family law, estate planning, and civil work will still have clients with mental health issues. Mental health issues can be anything from dementia or Alzheimer's to schizophrenia or any other number of conditions.

There are several things to keep in mind when dealing with clients with mental health issues. The first thing to remember is that you as the attorney must be extra patient. A client with mental health issues may need you to speak slower or to explain things several times. Be accommodating and try to make the client feel like you are being accommodating without talking down to them.

One other important thing to remember when dealing with clients with mental health issues is that they often have support people that may be helpful to you. By support people I mean family members, doctors, caseworkers, physiologists and anyone else that may be able to help. A lot of the time the client will tell you about the people helping them but other times you will have to find them on your own. Generally, when I have a client with mental health issues, I will ask them if they have a caseworker. The caseworker can often give me more information so that I can better assist the client. Always remember that even with clients with mental health issues there are confidentiality and privilege issues.

Difference Between Confidence and Arrogance

There is a big difference between an attorney being confident and arrogant. Confident means you know what you are doing because you have done it before. Confidence shows your clients and those around you that you are in control and that things will get handled in a professional matter. Confidence comes from doing things the right way over and over. From client management to trials to settlement conferences, confidence comes from experience. Being experienced doesn't automatically mean you are confident but like with all things experience helps.

Arrogance is what all lawyers must avoid. If confidence is letting your actions speak for you, arrogance is you speaking about your actions. Arrogance is telling support staff how awesome you are and how successful you are. Arrogance is one of the worst qualities any person can have but it is especially dangerous for attorneys. Unfortunately, many people expect lawyers to be arrogant. This is in part from how lawyers are portrayed in media but some of the fault also lies with attorneys. If a person expects you to be arrogant and you are then this confirms all the bad stereotypes.

Arrogance will also hurt your career. If you are arrogant and you don't think this will affect how a judge rules on your motion you are mistaken. If you don't think your arrogance will affect when the bailiff schedules your trial you are also mistaken. Imagine the following conversation:

> Arrogant lawyer: "Bailiff, I'm a big important lawyer and you are a support person, I am going on a fancy expensive vacation on the 15th so make sure my trial is NOT on that date, simple enough?"

Bailiff: "I will put you down for the 15th, and will make personally sure the Judge does not change that date."

Believe it or not I have seen attorneys talk to support staff in similar fashion. Arrogance will not only hurt you with judges and support staff but it will also hurt you with opposing counsel and prosecutors. If you go to a prosecutor and are arrogant why the hell would they offer your client a better deal or a deviation request? I have had clients ask me why I am so nice to prosecutors. I explain that it is in their best interest that I am nice to prosecutors because the nicer I am the less prison time they will get.

Arrogance seems to be especially a large problem with newer attorneys. I think that most experienced attorneys have figured out arrogance does not get them very far. I also think many new attorneys WRONGLY think that being attorneys makes them important and they can talk down to people and be arrogant. Remember that arrogance is part of your reputation and once your reputation is damaged it is incredibly hard if not impossible to fix.

Chapter 9

Dealing with Clients and Attorneys

A large part of any attorney's day is dealing with either clients or other attorneys. The other attorneys may be people in your office, prosecutors, opposing counsel or co-counsel. Being skillful in dealing with clients and other attorneys can be the difference between enjoying your work and hating it. An attorney who is good at dealing with others is easy to see. The opposite type of attorney is equally easy to see. Young attorneys often expect for clients to be difficult but are surprised how difficult other attorneys can be. My goal is to help young attorneys not only deal better with difficult clients but difficult attorneys as well.

The best and the worst part of being an attorney can be dealing with clients. There are few feelings better than when a client tells you what an amazing job you did and gives you a hug. There are fewer worse feelings than when a client tells you they are filing a bar complaint for some perceived injustice. Every attorney has stories of clients that have loved them and clients that have hated them. Lawyers provide a service to clients. Our goal is to make clients happy, but new attorneys must be realistic in that some clients will never be happy and nothing can be done about it. Sometimes it really is them and not you.

Clients and Setting Prices

One area where new attorneys (including me) have a hard time is in dealing with clients and money. Issues such as how much money to charge, when to collect money, when to sue a client, how to bill clients, and dealing with clients unhappy about how much they owe are difficult issues. One area that is important to a healthy practice is setting prices. When I started, I had a hard time setting prices because I had a bad habit of underquoting clients. If you underquote by a little bit it is no big deal but if you underquote by a lot it can be a large problem. After an attorney has been practicing for a while it is easy to know how much to charge. Before you figure out how much to charge you need to figure out if you will be charging a flat fee or an hourly fee. Your field of law will often dictate how you charge.

Some fields of law such as criminal law or estate planning are a lot more accustomed to flat fees. A flat fee is exactly what it sounds like. A client comes to you and says I want to hire you. You tell the client how much you will charge to handle the entire case. An hourly fee is the opposite and the attorney charges as they go. If you are doing civil work there is a good chance you will be billing hourly. If you are not sure if you should bill hourly or a flat fee, talk to other attorneys in the area and they will know. Other attorneys are also a great resource for help with setting fees. Even today when a client wants to hire me for a type of case I have not handled before I will call one of my attorney friends that has handled that type of case and ask them what they charge.

It is also important to get as much information from your potential client as possible before quoting them a price. I learned this lesson the hard way. I had a client call me and tell me he had a drug possession case. I falsely assumed he would be eligible for probation and told him I would do the case for $1500. This was my first mistake.

Generally you should not quote prices over the phone. Have the person come to your office and talk face to face. One attorney with over thirty years of experience told me he always has potential clients come to the office where he gives them his "eye brow test." He explained to me that when he tells them a price, if their eyebrows go up when they are shocked at how much he wants to charge he lowers the price. Remember you can always adjust your price down from your original quote but not the opposite. If you ask a client for five thousand dollars and they say no problem, you can't then say, "Well what about six thousand?"

After my potential client came in and hired me, he told me he had multiple felony prior convictions and was on felony probation for a felony less than two years ago. After doing a little research I figured out that he was looking at close to 20 years in prison. The mistake was entirely my own and I learned from it. I now have a checklist of questions that I ask potential clients. If they do not want to answer the questions this is a huge red flag and I do not want their business because they will be trouble down the road. Like with many other things, a little information up front can save a lot of trouble down the road. These are some of the questions I now ask all potential clients:

- Have they ever been charged with a crime before?
- Have they ever been convicted of a crime?

- Any felony or misdemeanor convictions?
- Are they on probation or parole?
- What court is this charge out of?
- How many total counts are there that they are being charged with?
- Have they spoken to other attorneys?
- Have they gotten price quotes from other attorneys?
- Has the defendant been to court on this charge yet?
- Will any motions be necessary?

Clients, Getting Money Up Front and Collecting Money Owed

You must get at least some money up front. Unless you have a client that you trust and know will pay, you must get some kind of money upfront. Getting money upfront is important for several reasons. The first is that it shows you that the client is serious about hiring you. It is very different when a client says they want to hire you and when they actually pay you. The second reason it is important to get money up front is because the client does not really appreciate your work until they have given you money. A client may say they appreciate your work but until they have given you money they do not really. Ask any attorney and they will tell you that they have heard every excuse possible as to why the client cannot pay them up front and if you start their case for free they will pay you soon. The following is only a partial list of reasons clients have told me about why they do not have money but will soon:

- Injury settlement money is coming in
- Money from a will or trust is coming to them
- Awaiting income tax return
- Parents will lend them the money
- Divorce settlement
- Payday is next week
- New business is taking off and will soon pay off
- Disability payment is in the mail
- Etc. . . .

How much money you get up front will depend on several variables. In criminal defense work we try to get as much money up front as we can. We know that often the money we get up front will be the only money we get. If you know this as an attorney this is not a problem, but if you think the client will pay more and they don't then it's a problem. The reason we know that often the money we get up front will be the only money we ever see is because many of our clients are less than honest. Many of our clients are in fact criminals.

Fee Agreements

You MUST have a written fee agreement. There are no exceptions. Many conflicts between attorneys and their clients could have been avoided if there had been a clear fee agreement. The fee agreement is necessary because it spells out what the attorney will and will not do and for how much. The fee agreement must also be clear if the fee is a flat fee and earned upon receipt or what the payment arrangement is. Most state bar websites will have a sample fee agreement and when you are new, it is not a bad idea to use the template.

It is important that the client not only sign the fee agreement but that you go over the agreement with them to make sure they clearly understand what they are, and are not, hiring you for. It is also important that your fee agreement either does or does not cover a trial. Some attorneys have a flat fee for the pretrial and trial parts of the case. Some attorneys have one fee for all the pretrial work and a separate fee for the trial. Obviously if a client thinks they are paying for everything but you plan on charging them a separate trial fee they will not be happy. A fee agreement should also cover if experts are necessary and approximately how much those experts can cost. I do a lot of DUI work and I have in my fee agreement a sentence that says that if the client wants an expert or the case requires an expert at trial that will be an extra fee and that the expert normally charges about $600 for the court appearance.

No matter how simple of a matter you are handling you must have a fee agreement. I recently handled a very simple matter for a client. They had old fines they owed to the court and they paid me to go to court with them to ask a judge to get rid of some of the fines. I went to court and asked and the judge said no. I thought that I had done everything that we had agreed to but the client thought otherwise. He thought that I would make as many court appearances as he wanted. The mistake was mine, as I did not have a fee agreement. If I had it, I could have avoided the confusion.

Client Management

While this is not a book on client management, the topic is important to discuss. For a more in-depth look at client management I would recommend my book called *Client Management for Lawyers*. Sorry for the shameless plug.

One of the best ways to manage clients, and keep clients from complaining and causing problems for you, is to manage their expectations. I have a friend who is a criminal defense attorney. He has been practicing law longer than I have been alive. He told me that when a client comes into his office he always tells them they are going to prison for a long, long time. After the client freaks out he says he will try to get them less prison. This is a very important lesson for all new attorneys. If you tell your client that they are facing a 10 on the disaster scale and the end result is a 7 they will be relatively happy. If you tell the client that they are facing a 2 on the disaster scale and the end result is a 4, they will think you didn't do a very good job and should have done more. It sounds strange, but I promise you this is true and you will see it for yourself.

Often new attorneys have a hard time with managing client expectations because they do not want to give the client bad news. You should not exaggerate the possible outcome but also be sure not to make the situation sound better than it actually is. Managing expectations is not only important for criminal defense attorneys, but all attorneys. Managing expectations is about more than just the outcome of the case.

Managing expectations also has to do with what the client expects of you. If the client thinks that they can call you ten times a day, late at night and on the weekends, you must be clear with them when you are available and when you are not. I know many attorneys that give out their cell phone numbers to clients. Many attorneys do not give out their cell phone numbers and tell their clients to call the office. Either approach is OK as long as the client knows what to expect.

Managing expectations is important from the first time you meet a prospective client. Setting the tone of the client-attorney relationship is just as important. The client must know that you are in charge and that they cannot push you around. Many clients will try to take advantage of inexperienced attorneys and tell them what to do and how to do it. You must always remember that you are the attorney and that the client came to you.

A client is always watching their attorney and deciding if the attorney knows what they are doing and if they should listen to them. If a client sees that you are in charge and in control, they are more likely to listen and your life will be easier. The opposite is also true. If a client senses that you are insecure in your work and how you carry yourself, they will take advantage of this and start thinking that they are in charge.

Clients generally do not understand if you are doing quality work, but they watch for things they do understand. I often tell students that how you say something is more important than what you say when speaking to a client. When you are explaining a complex legal theory to a client they will likely not understand. What the client will understand is your tone. Think of your dog or cat. A dog does not understand words but it understands tone. A dog understands whether someone speaking to it is confident, scared, or indecisive. Clients are often the same way.

Clients will listen for tone but they will also watch your actions. Clients see things like if you are on time or not. Clients see if your paperwork is ready when you come to court or if you are a disheveled mess. Clients see how you carry yourself with opposing counsel, with the prosecutor, or with the judge. I know many attorneys that are not very good at knowing the law but make a great presentation for their clients and the clients think they are the best attorneys in the world. Not all clients are the same and there are several types that you will see over and over.

One type of client you will encounter is a client that has never been to a lawyer. This type of client is common in any field of law. This type of client will often have a million questions and will require some handholding. I say hand holding figuratively but sometimes it will be literal. I once had a senior citizen female client that would grab on to my hand when walking into court. An attorney has to remember that many people have never met an attorney. Attorneys tend to forget this because it is our profession and we know many attorneys.

To many clients, meeting an attorney is intimidating and you must work to make the client comfortable. This type of client will often bring a small, or not so small, support system with them. I have seen clients bring their entire families to court for support. There is no problem with bringing people to court with them, but if they are coming to your office, you want to be clear with them how having people there affects the attorney-client privilege. Clients that have never used an attorney before are generally easier to manage than the next type of client.

Frequent flier clients are present in every field of law. In civil practice, they may be always trying to sue current or former business partners. In the criminal world they are clients that are always getting in trouble for one thing or another. The advantage of frequent flier clients is that they generally know what to expect. They have been to court before and know what to expect in court. These types of clients also know how much legal services cost. If the client has hired you before, you will have a working relationship with them, which will make the handing of their case easier.

The downside of frequent flier clients is that they often think they know more than you. They may try telling you what to do and often think that their legal experience entitles them to an honorary law degree. Every client is different and there are no blanket rules, but frequent flier clients are generally pushier than clients that have never used an attorney before. With frequent flier clients it is crucial that you establish that you are in charge.

I once had a client who was charged with a DUI. This was his second or third DUI and he thought he knew the law. The problem with his case was that he hit a parked police cruiser while the officer watched him hit his car. Needless to say the client was very drunk as he drove into the police car. The client was trying to tell me that the officer had to have probable cause to stop him and he had none and the case should be thrown out. There is nothing more dangerous than a client who thinks they know the law.

Another type of client that you will have is the habitual liar. They will lie about anything and everything and not think twice about it. I have had these clients and I can be watching a video of them shoplifting and they will sit in front of me and tell me that they were not shoplifting. When I tell them I am watching a video that they are also watching showing them shoplifting they will tell me that it is not them.

With habitual liar clients, is important that you not believe anything they tell you. You must verify everything and not go off anything they tell you. The good thing about these clients is that they lie so much that it is usually fairly easy to catch on and act accordingly. If you figure out that they are lying about everything before they hire you, you may not want their business. If the client will be more of headache than they are worth, you may not want them to hire you.

Just several days ago, I had a trial with a client that was a frequent flier and a habitual liar. He was in his mid-40s and had been to prison several times. In his current case, he went over to his neighbor's and started peeing on his front door. When the neighbor opened the door, my drunken defendant attacked the neighbor. At the trial, three officers testified that my client was incredibly drunk and all three officers saw a bottle of vodka in his hands. The neighbor also testified and said he knew the defendant well from other incidents in the complex and he clearly recognized my client. My client testified and said he never drinks alcohol, was not drinking on the night in question, and didn't pee on anyone's door. After he was convicted, he started yelling that he wanted an appeal.

The last type of client worth mentioning is the client that is mad at the world. They can be any age and think nothing is their fault and that the world is out to get them. These types of clients are almost never happy and virtually impossible to make happy. If they are going to hire you, you need to know from the start that they are not likely to end up happy. No matter the type of law you practice you will have clients that are mad at the world. You can usually see these clients from a mile away. They will complain about everything and blame everyone.

An attorney must always be in charge, and with this type of client it is crucial that the attorney make it clear they are in charge. This type of client will blame you for everything that they can. This is what they do. Clients that are mad at the world are usually jaded about everything and their attitude reflects their outlook. Ultimately no matter the type of client you have you must build trust with them. No matter if your client is crazy, a liar, aggressive, or perfectly normal, your life will be a lot easier and the representation will go much smoother if the client trusts you.

Trust must be built. Clients want to know that you as their attorney tried for them and fought for them. A lot of my criminal defense court-appointed clients have never had anyone in a suit fight for them. When they see an attorney fighting for them and doing everything they can to help them they will be grateful. With any relationship trust is hard to build and easy to lose.

If you tell a client you will call them on a certain day you must call them on that certain day. If you promise something to your client you must deliver on that promise. If you break a promise to a client they will not only remember it but they will tell other people how their attorney let them down. This is not only bad for your own reputation, but also for the reputation of attorneys in general. An attorney must never forget that a client trusts them to handle something very important to the client. Whether it is a criminal case, a divorce, a lawsuit or any other legal matter, that matter is of great importance to the client.

I recently had an Ethiopian client who was charged with a DUI. At first he was not very trusting and told me that back home most attorneys and police are corrupt and that no one had ever really fought for him. He was a court-appointed client so he falsely assumed I would not try very hard for him. He assumed he would be found guilty and I told him I would do everything I could for him.

After a multiple day jury trial, the jury was deadlocked and the judge declared a mistrial. After the prosecutor refiled the charges we had a second jury trial. After another multiple-day trial the jury was out for hours but came back with a guilty verdict. The client was very upset about the verdict, but told me that I had done more for him than he ever thought an attorney would. This is how attorneys build trust with clients.

Dealing with Difficult Clients

You will have difficult clients. This is a reality and every attorney will tell you they have difficult clients. There are several things a new attorney must understand about some difficult clients. Many difficult clients will never be happy and new attorneys must understand that. No matter how hard their attorney tries for them, they will never be happy. New attorneys must understand that often when the client is unhappy it is not about what the attorney did but about other things in the difficult client's life. Difficult clients will often not listen at all. They will put blame everywhere they can but never on themselves.

I once had a client who was charged with pointing a gun at a small child outside of his apartment window. We had a trial and many witnesses testified they saw my client point the gun out of his window. All the witnesses were credible and all told the exact same story. As expected, my client was convicted and as expected he took no responsibility for his actions. After the trial he told me that maybe if I had done a better job he would not have been found guilty. This is a typical difficult client.

Another client I recently had also demonstrates how difficult clients typically are. I knew the client was going to be difficult before I ever met him. He had been reassigned to me from a different attorney. That attorney had withdrawn because the client kept calling his office and kept yelling at the entire staff. The client was in his late 70s and was arrested for telling the people at the food stamp office that he was going to kill everyone there. He was mad because his food stamp benefits had been reduced.

When I met with him, he told me he wanted a trial and that he was innocent. I told him they had him on video threating to kill people. He told me that did not prove anything. I told him it proved the charge he was charged with. Eventually I got him no jail time and he pled guilty but he always maintained he did nothing wrong. No matter how difficult a client is an attorney must always remain professional.

Often clients have their own theories and it can be difficult to explain things to them. Another memorable client was charged with a DUI after he had run into a parked police car. Not only had he run into a parked police car he did so while the officer stood next to his car while it was being run into. When I met with the client he told me he was only being prosecuted because the police and prosecutors are racist because he is black. I tried to explain to him that he was being prosecuted because he ran into a parked cop car while very, very drunk. I had to remain calm and professional and explain the reality of the situation to him. Eventually the defendant came around and realized that his best bet would be to plead guilty.

Not Judging Your Clients

An attorney must always remember not to judge their clients. This is not to say you can't go home and tell your wife or husband about your crazy client and how terrible they are. I do that all the time and my friends look forward to hearing about my clients. When I say you can't judge your client, I mean you can't judge them to their face. Often clients are embarrassed or scared when talking to an attorney and you must always be aware of this. A good attorney must try to make their client more comfortable.

A young attorney, who is no longer doing defense work, once met with a client and did something a defense attorney should never do. After the client told them what happened, the attorney told them what they did was stupid. It should be clear why this person is no longer practicing defense work. I once represented a young lady who was charged with a DUI. There is nothing unusual about someone being charged with a DUI. The unusual thing about her case was that she was so drunk she called the police on herself.

The woman had not only called the police on herself for drunk driving, she did so while naked in her car. At the time the police showed up she was parked in the middle of the intersection totally naked. When the police arrested her and put her in the back of the police car she peed herself. When I was talking to her she was obviously very embarrassed. Part of being a professional is to make clients feel comfortable and not to embarrass them any further. Even though I was laughing to myself about someone being so drunk that they called the police on themselves, I had to protect to the client's feelings. The following examples are a few of my cases where I had to work hard to not judge my clients.

I had another client who was charged with prostitution. She happened to be married to her pimp (the family that works together stays together). She wanted him to sit in on our consultation. The woman was so unattractive that the undercover police officer had a difficult time soliciting her for her services. I had to read the entire police report to this woman with a straight face. Again, I wanted to laugh at how ridiculous the situation was but obviously as an attorney I had to stay composed.

Another one of my memorable clients was arrested for assault after slapping her husband. What was memorable about this case was that she slapped him during group sex gone wrong. My defendant and her husband met another couple at a hotel and went to a room to have group sex. As my defendant's husband was having sex with the other woman the condom broke. The husband told his wife not to worry as he had had a vasectomy. The other woman chimed in that she had had a hysterectomy. At this point my defendant freaked out and slapped her husband who quickly called the police on his own wife.

I can't tell you how hard it is to keep a straight face when reading such a jewel of a police report. I remember thinking about what the police were thinking when they showed up to the hotel and found four naked people in a hotel room. While I was reading the police report to the woman she was obviously horribly embarrassed. Imagine how horrified and embarrassed she would have been if I said, "Wow, what the hell were you thinking?" I did not say anything to her not related to the case and as we talked she saw I was being professional, and over time she calmed down and felt more comfortable.

Clients with Mental Health Issues

Generally, when people think of clients with mental health issues they think of criminal defense attorneys. While defense attorneys do deal with such clients they are not the only attorneys. Civil attorneys ranging from personal injury attorneys to estate planning attorneys must also deal with clients with mental health issues. Some clients, or sometimes their families, will tell you about their issues, sometimes they will be obvious, and yet other times they will not be obvious at first but will reveal themselves over time.

There are a couple of things to remember when dealing with clients with mental health issues. First, try to treat the client like you would any client to the extent possible. Sometimes treating the client the same as other clients will not be possible. Again, your goal should be to treat the client as close to normal as possible. The client will appreciate you treating them normally whenever possible. Remember with any client your goal is to earn their trust.

Something else to remember about clients with mental health issues is that as part of your service you may want to get them additional resources. What I mean by this is that there may be agencies that can provide support to your client that they may not know about. No one expects you to be an expert on helping clients with mental health issues but the more you can do for your client the happier they will be.

Too Much Empathy vs. Being Cold/Not Caring At All

A good attorney has to be able to balance having empathy for their clients with protecting their own emotions. There are attorneys that go too far on both extremes. There are attorneys that are completely consumed with their clients and their needs. They take on all the emotions of their clients' cases and over time they become burned out. A typical defense attorney will hear hundreds, if not thousands, of sad, heartbreaking stories every year. If that attorney takes on all that sadness as his or her own, it can be difficult to deal with.

The other extreme is attorneys who do not care at all. A client will tell them that they just had a child die and the attorney will say that is not my problem. These attorneys do a great deal of harm to their clients as the clients are often looking for someone to listen to them. That attorney pushes the client away when the client needs someone to listen to them the most. The key is balance.

There is no secret to balancing empathy with not caring at all. Many attorneys go their whole career without ever learning how to do it. Most attorneys learn to balance the two with time. When I started I was closer to the caring too much end of the spectrum. I have learned to protect myself emotionally while still caring and listening to clients.

A good attorney must always remember that the client is there because they need your help. Most times when an attorney has a client sitting in front of them it is one of the lowest points of the client's life. The client might be facing jail, divorce, a lawsuit, a bankruptcy, business trouble, or other problems. You must protect yourself emotionally but not become completely cold to your clients.

Dealing with Difficult Attorneys

> "If it doesn't make you money or make you happy, don't do it."
> — Adam Carolla

Just as I can assure you will have difficult clients, I can assure you will have to deal with difficult attorneys. They may be opposing counsel, prosecutors or other attorneys in your field. There are a million reasons why attorneys are difficult to other attorneys. Some are naturally that way. Some are burned-out and angry at the world. Some will be difficult to other attorneys as a strategy (not a very good strategy, but still a strategy).

I have had to deal with many difficult attorneys, but one stands out. I got a call from the court asking me if I could cover for another attorney. The person who was supposed to cover had double-booked and the court needed my help. The court told me to bill the attorney so I did. After not paying me for close to a month the attorney told me I was charging him too much. I told him I was charging my regular rate and was not charging him anything extra. The attorney then sent me a letter that he would not be using me for coverage any-more and that he was telling other attorneys not to hire me. I wanted to re-spond, but I chose to take the high road.

Some attorneys will be difficult to deal with directly. I have seen attorneys throw papers at prosecutors, yell at prosecutors, and have outbursts in court. Some attorneys will be difficult in weird passive aggressive ways, like writing crappy emails or by not paying for your work on time. You cannot control how other attorneys behave but you can control how you react. I have had to deal with several unprofessional and difficult attorneys and I have always tried to take the high road. I have wanted to write back emails and call people names and confront people but I always remembered the great American philoso-pher, Adam Carolla.

He once said something that I have thought about often and shared with a lot of people. He said that every time he deals with someone difficult and wants to retaliate and respond, he asks himself if his response will make him happy or make him money? If the answer is no, then don't do it. Sounds simple, but like everything it takes practice.

Dealing with People That Don't Like You

No matter how nice, friendly, professional and likeable you are there will be clients, attorneys, judges, and court staff that do not like you. This is a real-ity that all new attorneys must face. When I started my own practice I went out of my way to be nice to everyone I could. Despite this there was one at-torney who was telling people I was stealing clients from other attorneys. Of course this was completely not true but she was still telling people this. Some other attorneys told me that the attorney talking about me did not like me. She didn't really have a good reason for not liking me but she still didn't.

There are a million reasons why someone might not like you. You can do your best to be likeable but there will always be some people that dislike you. Often the reason is trivial and silly. I have had female attorneys tell me they did not like another female attorney because they did not like how she dressed. Someone may not like you because the person who has a problem with you is unhappy and is projecting on to you. Sometimes people's personalities clash and there is very little that can be done.

The key to dealing with people that do not like you is to remain profes-sional. If you begin to be unprofessional this will only give the person you do not like more ammunition. Depending on how confrontational you are you can always talk to the person who doesn't like you. By taking a direct approach you might be able to work out the disagreement. If the person who doesn't like you is not open to resolving the issue, talking to them will probably help little. Just remember that there will be people that you work with that will not like you and to remain professional.

Chapter 10

Managing Your Practice

Managing Your Money

How you manage money will determine if your practice survives or fails. It doesn't matter how good your reputation is, or how many cases you win, or how much clients like you if you are out of money. It always amazes me how many attorneys are terrible at managing money. Some attorneys are excellent at making money, but because they do not know how to manage it they run into problems.

From buying expensive cars to expensive toys and trips, attorneys are excellent at blowing money. Many attorneys get into trouble with money in the same way as many professional athletes. If an attorney gets a new car, the other attorney in his office may want to get an even more expensive car to show off and to compete with the attorney. If one attorney has two homes, someone else will want three. One good way to manage your money is to keep track of where it goes and how much you are actually making.

One good way to manage money is to use good accounting software. I have always used QuickBooks Online and would recommend it to new attorneys. The program is simple to use and does a great job of tracking who owes you money and your spending patterns. It doesn't matter if you use QuickBooks or another program, but you must keep track of your expenses. I can easily check to see how much I spent on my car last year or last month, or how much money I spent on eating out, or the cost of my monthly utilities. A business cannot control expenses if it doesn't know what those expenses are.

Another great feature about QuickBooks is that I can easily see who owes me money and if I owe anyone money. Not only will the program tell me who owes me money it will tell me how late they are in paying. I can organize outstanding invoices by date so I know who I need to worry about getting paid from, because their invoice is the oldest. I have been using QuickBooks for four years and I am still discovering cool features that I did not know about.

At the end of every day I input receipts. Since the program is online, at the end of the year all my CPA has to do in log on to my account with the temporary password that I give him and prepare my taxes. The program being online is convenient for more than just end-of-year tax purposes. If I ever have a question about one of my accounts or want my CPA to look at something all he has to do is log on. I am always amazed how many attorneys still have a shoebox full of receipts that they take to their CPA at the end of the year. Actually I am amazed how many attorneys don't have a CPA.

This brings me to the next important aspect of managing money. Get a good CPA. With CPAs, like with all professionals, you get what you pay for. If your CPA charges ten bucks an hour, but works out of his car, you are likely to go to prison for tax evasion. My CPA is not cheap, but I know he does good work. For me, paying him well is worth it because I know that my taxes will be done correctly and if there is ever a problem he will be there to help. I knew nothing about taxes when I started, so I knew that it would be important to have a professional helping me.

I am often amazed how many attorneys do not have separate accounts for their business and their personal accounts. You should be very careful to keep your personal accounts separate from your business accounts. Do not use a personal credit card for business purchases. Do not use business checks to pay for personal expenses. Make sure that your online personal bank account is not linked to your business bank account. If you have a personal credit card and a business credit card make sure they are different colors so you don't use the wrong one by accident. Also make sure your personal and business checks are different colors so you don't accidently confuse them.

Another good way to manage money is to not spend a lot of it. A lot of young attorneys fail at having their own practice not because they are bad attorneys but because their spending is greater than their income. This problem is not unique to new attorneys. I know attorneys that make huge amounts of money but manage to spend even more, and as a result they are still broke. If you make a half a million dollars a year but spend a half million dollars plus one dollar you are still broke.

Many attorneys are drawn to expensive offices, expensive cars and an expensive lifestyle. Often this is a quick way to go broke. A good example is a car payment. If your payments are $300 a month instead of $600 a month that's an extra $3,600 in your pocket over a year. Over five years the savings would be $18,000. Now for the real savings. If you don't have a car payment at all that's an extra $18,000 dollars in your pocket. Do you want a new car or an extra $18,000?

Little expenses can add up too. Instead of eating out for lunch every day consider bringing a bag lunch. If an attorney eats out every day that is approximately $200 a month. Over a year the total is $2,400, and over five years the total climbs $12,000. The lesson is simple; if you bring lunch from home you will save $12,000 dollars. Obviously you will eat out sometimes, but think of how much money you will save. I know many attorneys that eat out every day and I often think of how much the lunches are costing them.

Try to save money in every place possible. Think of things like your gas mileage. If you drive a lot, having a car with excellent gas mileage can a big difference. Last year I drove over 21,000 miles traveling between different courts. If I drove a car that got terrible gas mileage, I would have paid thousands of dollars more for gas than I had to. The point is not that you have to sell your car and buy a hybrid, but that you must be creative in trying to save money.

One other place where you may be able to save money is by having a cell phone instead of a landline. A traditional office line setup can cost hundreds of dollars a month. A simple cell phone can be purchased relatively cheaply, and you can get unlimited minutes for as little as twenty dollars a month. Remember, when a client calls you they don't know if you have a fancy office setup or a cheap cell phone. A cell phone also has the added benefit of being portable.

Another important part of managing your money is deciding what forms of payment you will accept. I always require that new clients either get cash or a money order or a cashier's check. If you know or trust the client a check can be acceptable. Be careful with checks, as they are often bad and will bounce. I once had a client charged with felony check fraud try to pay me with a check. Credit cards are convenient and a good option for clients, as clients often do not have enough money in their bank accounts to pay.

There are several things to watch out for with credit cards. First, be careful what the credit card company or the bank is charging you in fees. Normally you should expect to pay somewhere around two to three percent per transaction. Watch out for hidden bank fees and transaction fees that may be buried in small print in your bank statement. The second thing to watch out for with credit cards is the challenge period. A person paying with a credit card has a certain amount of time to challenge the transaction. This is important to you because after a client pays you they can challenge the transaction and the credit card company can put a hold on the transaction or ask for the money back. The bottom line with credit cards is to be careful.

The last and perhaps most important aspect of managing money is to have cash saved up. The more cash you have on hand the more comfortable you will feel. When you have a big payday from a client or a settlement, hold on to as much of that money as possible. If you have a slow month, having cash saved up can be the difference between your practice surviving or closing.

Insurance

An important part of managing your practice is having adequate insurance. There are several types of insurance that you need to have. You must have malpractice insurance. Not you should have malpractice insurance, you MUST have malpractice insurance. Malpractice insurance is one of those things that you hope you never need, but when you do need it can save your practice. A surprising number of attorneys do not have malpractice insurance as a cost-cutting measure. I once spoke to an attorney that chose not to have malpractice insurance so he could afford a fancier office. At first I thought he was joking, but he was not.

How much you pay for malpractice insurance will depend on several factors. The first is how long you have been practicing. Insurance providers figure the longer you have been practicing the more clients you will have had. The more clients you have/had the more likely that one of them will sue you. Malpractice insurance usually gets more expensive every year. The increase in price is gradual but continues. The second factor that will determine how much you pay is the type of law you practice.

Attorneys in different areas of law are charged different amounts. The reason is that attorneys in certain types of law are more likely to have claims for money brought against them. If a criminal defense attorney screws up a client's case may be overturned. The client is not likely to win money so the insurance company won't have to pay anything. If a personal injury attorney screws up, the insurance company can be out a lot of money.

For example, if a personal injury attorney misses the statute of limitations on a client's case and the client sues for malpractice, the insurance company will be writing a check. Since a personal injury attorney is more likely to cost the insurance company more money, they are charged more. When I first began to look for malpractice insurance I was told that criminal defense attorneys have some of the lowest premiums while personal injury attorneys have the highest.

Make sure you shop around for the best price. This was one of the many lessons I learned the hard way. My first year in practice I went with a provider that I saw advertise in Arizona State Bar Magazine. The price sounded reasonable so I went with them. I did not shop around and just accepted their price. When it was time to renew I shopped around and found the same policy for $200 dollars less. Remember, every penny counts. Also, keep in mind that the first couple of years you will not have a lot of clients so you are less likely to need the insurance. Get a sufficient amount of coverage, but you will not likely need millions of dollars of coverage. Obviously, the more coverage you have the more you will pay in premiums. Malpractice insurance is a good start, but not the only type of insurance you should have.

You need to have health insurance. The reason is simple. If you get sick or need surgery the cost could wipe you out. One surgery could cost hundreds of thousands of dollars. I would recommend a very basic base policy. Most of the policies have the word catastrophic or emergency coverage (comforting, I know). The good thing about health insurance is that if you are relatively young and healthy a basic policy will not cost very much. Like with everything else remember to shop around. The difference in price between two similar policies can be huge. You need health insurance but there is a third type of insurance to consider.

Many young attorneys do not have disability insurance but they should. If you don't know what disability insurance is think of the Aflac duck. If you are not able to work, the policy pays you a preset amount for a preset amount of time. The reason young attorneys should consider this type of insurance is because when you operate a solo firm everything is on you. If you are not able to work you will have to hire someone to go to court. You will also need a way to pay the bills. If I am not working I am not making money. The chances of something happening to you so you are not able to work are low but this does not mean you should not plan for it. The good thing about disability insurance is that it is very cheap. A reasonable policy can be bought for $30–40 a month. A good way to learn about any type of insurance is to speak with a broker that can answer all your questions about different types of policies.

Files

Keeping good files is essential. Keeping a good file is not difficult, but many attorneys do not do it. I am always amazed when I see some attorney pull a wad of papers out of their suitcase and try to figure out what paper is what. There are a million different systems for filing, and I'm not sure there is a correct one or a wrong one. Some people will keep their files in an alphabetical order, others by chronological order. Some people will design their own system with code letters and code numbers. Whatever system you use be consistent and start using the system right away. When you only have three clients, keeping track of their files will not be difficult. But once you have 300 or 3,000 files, you will have to find the correct files while you are running out the door, late to court.

Keeping a neat updated file is just as important as a good file organization system. A long time ago when I was interning at the Washtenaw County Public Defender's Office in Ann Arbor, Michigan, I had a boss there that had a rule that I still follow. He told us that any time we picked up a file to note what we did with it. He told us that if we were hit by a bus, another attorney should be able to pick up the file and know everything that had been done up to that point. I will give you the same advice. Every time you pick up a file for any reason, note what you did in the file. You don't have to go into great length but make a note.

If you look through the file, if you call the client, if you prepare a motion — any time you do anything make a note. This is an important practice for several reasons. The first reason is that unavoidably you will have a client who tries to throw you under the bus and complain to someone that you have not done any work. The unhappy client will complain to a judge or the state bar. This is the time you will be glad that you kept a good file.

I once had a client that was the classic difficult client. Nothing was ever her fault and everyone else was to blame. She had received over twenty speeding tickets in less than two years and now had a reckless driving and criminal speeding charge. She drew the attention of the officers following her as she was going in excess of eighty miles an hour weaving in and out of traffic while applying make-up with both hands. She had gotten so many speeding tickets in one area that when the officer pulled her over, he recognized her from when he had cited her two weeks ago.

I told her we did not have a good case for trial as the police had recorded the entire sequence of events and that the video clearly showed her not only speeding, but driving dangerously. She was not happy with what I had to say so she approached the judge and told her she wanted a different defense attorney, stating I had not done anything and had not returned her phone calls. Fortunately for me, I had kept a good record in the file. I read to the judge all the dates I had met with this client, all the times I had called her, all the times I had emailed and all other dates I had worked on her case. When I was done the judge turned to the defendant and said, "It seems like Mr. Benikov has done quite a bit for you." The defendant never complained about me again.

Properly closing out a file is just as important as keeping an organized file. When you are done with a client and their case is concluded you need to have a system for closing out their file. The system can be as simple as looking through the file and making sure everything has been done correctly. Some attorneys mail the client a letter telling them that the representation in the matter has ended. This is a good idea so that the client clearly understands that attorney is no longer representing them.

Once you close out the file you must keep it for a certain amount of time. Different states have different rules for how long attorneys must keep a closed file. Make sure you know what the rules are in your state and that you comply. Once the proper amount of time has gone by you can throw the file out, but make sure that everything is properly shredded.

Letterhead, Business Cards, and Websites

The reason I have all three categories in one section is because they are all a reflection of your practice. Often before a client meets you in person they will see your business card or your website. A good business card is kind of like good service at a restaurant. When the service is good most people don't notice, but when the service is bad it is very obvious. I have seen a lot of bad attorney business cards. I have seen ones that look like they should belong to a clown doing kid's birthday parties. I have seen cards without an address. When I see a card without an address, I assume the attorney is working out of their car. I have seen business cards with cartoon font or text that is illegible. When picking out a card, there are a few things to consider.

The font has to be big enough to be clearly seen. If you are doing estate planning or any field where your clients are going to be older you will want a larger font. The font will often look bigger on the computer than it will on the actual card. You will want to get a sample of the card to see how the font actually looks. I learned this the hard way when I got my first cards made. When the printer and I designed them, they looked like a good size, but when they were delivered to me the contact information was way too small and hard to read.

Something else to keep in mind with the cards is that you get what you pay for. If you go online and do one of those free card deals you will get your money's worth. Good cards will cost more, but they will look better. A decent printer will give you cards that are sturdy and have nice ink and look presentable. One other thing to think about with cards is a logo.

One of the most common logos for attorneys is a scale. When I designed my first cards I specifically did not use a scale. I thought they were passé and only something old attorneys used. I have kind of come around on scales. They are an easy way for people to know you are an attorney. Remember, a lot of people do not know a lot about attorneys but everyone knows a scale means you are an attorney. One idea to consider is designing your own scale. With your own design you still get a scale but it will look different than everyone else's. Remember your cards are a reflection of you and you want to make the best impression possible. Same thing goes for letterhead.

You want letterhead that makes a good impression. You want letterhead that says it belongs to an attorney that is doing well (even if you are not). Whether attorneys like it or not, presentation is a large part of our business. The quality of letterhead and business cards will be partially determined by the clients you are trying to attract. If most of your clients are court appointed or low income, they don't care what your letterhead looks like. Most of them will not know what letterhead is and don't care to know. On the other hand, if you are trying to attract wealthy clients or business professionals they will expect quality letterhead and business cards. Also, it is important that your letterhead and business cards match.

One last thing worth thinking about when it comes to letterhead is having your own greeting cards. Having personalized greeting cards to say thank you or to wish people happy holidays could be a great tool for generating business. People remember actual cards they receive a lot more than an email. When another attorney sends you a client and you send them a personalized card thanking them they will remember the gesture. When I receive a greeting card for the holidays or for my birthday from a fellow attorney I am more likely to give them referrals as I will be reminded of them. If a client receives a birthday card from you they will be happy.

One attorney that I spoke with has told me he has gotten many referrals from clients after sending them a greeting card. There are now services that will mail cards from you automatically on preset dates. Obviously, you will have to pay for the cards and postage, but as the old adage goes you have to spend money to make money.

The key to getting good letterhead and business cards is to find a good printer. I go to a little print shop that is owned by a friend. The prices are higher than a big box printer, but the work is better quality. You can find a quality printer in any town. A good printer will take the time to design the stationary with you and make sure that the final product turns out well. Again, remember you get what you pay for.

Websites are one of the most popular topics of discussion for attorneys. Like many topics that attorneys love to discuss, there are several schools of thought. Some attorneys, mostly older ones, will tell you that you do not need a website. These attorneys will tell you that there is nothing wrong with a phone. Some attorneys will tell you that in order to attract any new clients to your website you have to spend a lot of money to make your website more visible and marketable. Opponents of websites will tell you that there are so many attorney websites that no one will ever find yours. This school of thought makes some valid points. For your website to come up first when someone searches a type of law is incredibly expensive.

Google and other companies make fortunes off Internet searches. For those that don't know how it works, the more you pay a search engine the more visible your website becomes. If you are not paying a search engine your website will come up on page 42,000 of the search results. If you are not paying to advertise your site the only way anyone will find your site is if they either enter your exact address or search for the exact website name.

One of the other schools of thoughts swears by websites and will tell you how they receive large amounts of their clients off the Internet. These attorneys will tell you that you must have a website and that every attorney needs one. Today I think an attorney must have a website, but not only for the purposes of attracting clients.

When I started my website I would not get many clients from the website, but I have a lot of clients that tell me that either they were referred to me and checked out my website before deciding to hire me. I have also current clients that checked out my website to find out more about my practice. The front page of my website has about forty or so case results from the last couple of years. Clients have told me that they like the list because it shows I handle a lot of cases and have gotten good results.

There are a million ways to do a website and very few of them are wrong. I do caution young attorneys that it is better to not have a website than to have a bad website. A potential client will probably not be turned off if you do not have a website but may be turned off if you have a bad website. I have seen a lot of terrible websites. If you know how to design your own website there is nothing wrong with doing it yourself. If you have no idea what you are doing and have no artistic ability you should think about letting someone else design your website.

There are many different schools of thought as to what should actually be on the website. Some basics are a must. There needs to be a description of the practice to tell potential clients what kind of practice you are running. If someone is looking for a divorce attorney, they need to know that you handle divorces. There also needs to be a description of you as a lawyer. This may be a picture, a bio, or a description. You also need to have contact info so potential clients know how to get a hold of you. I recommend an email option, as some people prefer email to telephone.

How much actual content you provide on the website is up to you. I have had clients tell me they like simple websites with very little content, while other clients have told me they like lawyer websites with tons of content. Personally I prefer a simpler, cleaner website that has more basic information.

I have designed my own website to include the following sections. I have client testimonials on my website because all the research out there on websites tells us that reviews from other clients are important to potential clients. Even if the potential client doesn't know the person who left a review, that review is important to them. I also have a section on past case results. The section lists over 100 different case results that I have won for my clients. Some of the cases are listed as trial wins, while others give a brief description of a reduced sentence or punishment I was able to secure for a client. This should be obvious but remember not to include the client's full name for confidentiality reasons.

I think a past case result section is important for a lawyer website for two reasons. First, potential clients want to see that the lawyer they are thinking about hiring is able to get good results for their past clients. Every potential client is hoping that their lawyer will be able to achieve a great outcome for them whether that outcome is settling a case, a better plea offer, or anything else that helps the client. The second reason the section is important is that potential clients want a lawyer that is busy. No potential client wants to look at a lawyer's website and see that they have handled one small matter in the past ten years. As the old saying goes, no one wants to eat in an empty restaurant.

Most lawyer website design experts will tell you that your website should have a blog. I agree with them for two reasons. First, a blog can help with search engine optimization. For example, if you have written a blog about reinstating your driver's license and someone is looking up how to reinstate their license your blog post might pop up. The second reason I like blogs is because they help create the impression that you know what you are talking about. If a potential client is looking for a divorce lawyer and you have well-written blog posts about different aspects of getting a divorce this gives the potential client the feeling that you really do know about divorces.

One other feature to consider when planning a website is an instant chat feature. There are many different types but essentially they allow a potential client to speak with someone right away by typing a message while visiting the website. Some of these are set up where the message goes to an answering service, while others are designed for the potential client to speak directly with a lawyer. While many large companies have such a feature many small law firms do not. Many clients like this feature because they can talk to a live person right away. Always remember that when a potential client is looking for a lawyer they need a lawyer's help right away, not a week from now.

A professional web designer will charge thousands of dollars to design a website. Consider asking your friends to see if they know how to build a website. Be careful who you let mess with your website. I had a friend who told me he knew what he was doing and then my email stopped working for three days. If you don't have a friend that can *competently* build you a website consider contacting the local art college or design school and seeing if a student will do it for a couple hundred bucks. As far as hosting, the website companies like GoDaddy will host a simple site for ten to twenty dollars a year.

Don't be afraid to try services that help with website design. If you don't have a ton of money to pay a local website designer, consider websites that can match you up with freelance website designers that will charge you less than local website designers.

One site that I have used many times, and would recommend, is Elance .com. After you create a profile you set a budget of how much you want to pay for a website design and then freelance web design people from around the world bid on your project. You can set an hourly price you are willing to pay or you can set a flat price. I recommend a flat price because that way there is no surprises. I have also used Elance for other projects such as logos, editing, and design projects. Another advantage of Elance is that the money you pay goes into an escrow account and you only release the payment to your designer once you are satisfied with their work.

Business Bank Accounts

You must have at least one business account. The money in that account should only be for and from the business. Never deposit money from the business into your private account. There are several reasons not to do this and one of them is for tax purposes. If you are audited, you do not want to have to explain to the IRS why you deposited business money into a personal account or vice versa. Many banks have free business accounts. There is no reason for you to be paying the bank to have the account. Many banks want you to open your business account at their bank, so you should ask what incentives the bank offers for new accounts. The incentives can be anything from a free safe deposit box to a couple hundred dollars in cash.

Make sure you know what the rules are in your state for attorney trust accounts. An attorney trust account is where an attorney must deposit money that belongs to the client or is not yet earned by the attorney. Even though the money is in the attorney's account, it belongs to the client. Many states do not require attorneys to have trust accounts, but some do. For example, in Arizona, a client's money that is not yet earned must go into something called an IOLTA account. IOLTA stands for Interest On Lawyer Trust Account. The interest from these accounts does not go to the client or the attorney but instead goes to a charitable organization fund run by the state bar.

Rules for maintaining trust accounts are very complicated. Many attorneys get themselves in trouble for not properly maintaining the accounts because they do not follow the rules. In Arizona, every year a number of attorneys get themselves in trouble with the bar by either comingling funds or not properly keeping records of the account. Make sure you check the rules for your state and learn them. Often state bars will offer continuing legal education classes on maintaining a trust account. If you are not required have to have a trust account I would recommend you not have one. I do not have one as I only do criminal defense work and my fees are earned upon receipt.

Technology

Technology is one of the few places where a new attorney can have an advantage over an older, more experienced attorney. It is no secret that technology advances at an amazing rate and a good lawyer should be aware of the latest technologies and how they can help their practice. I'm not saying a lawyer's day should be consumed with knowing everything occurring in the tech world, but staying afloat of what can help a practice is beneficial. Chances are, a new attorney will be more comfortable with technological advances and will be more likely to use the technology. Simply knowing of a technology and actually integrating the technology into a practice are two very different things. I recently had an older attorney ask me if I knew what PowerPoint was and how it worked. I have been using PowerPoint for presentations since high school. He had more experience than me, but he didn't know what PowerPoint was. Using technological advances in your practice can give you an advantage, make your life easier, and make your practice run smoother. One of the biggest advances in technology in the last couple of years has been smartphones.

Today, from my phone, I can check my schedule, pull up a file, check a court docket, deposit a check, see who owes me money, or scan a document. Even a couple of years ago, many of these technologies did not exist. I am sure two years from now my phone will be able to do things that I can't even imagine today. New attorneys should become familiar and comfortable with all the things their phones can do. Here are a few basic suggestions for getting the most out of your phone.

You must have a smartphone. Your smartphone must be hooked up to your email. When a court or potential client is trying to reach you by email, you must be available. If you are only getting emails at your office, you will likely miss out on opportunities. I have signed up more than one client while vacationing out of the country. If a potential client is not able to get a hold of you over email or phone they will go to the next lawyer and you will have lost a client.

One of the biggest tech advances over the last couple of years has been the ability to take a credit card payment from a smartphone. Before this technology was available a lawyer would have to rent or buy a credit card processing machine from the bank. Before that an actual copy of the credit card had to be made each transaction. Today a lawyer can either swipe a credit card with their phone or take a credit card number over the phone. As with everything, when choosing a credit card processing service, shop around. Different companies will have different processing fees. Today most of the big companies don't charge a monthly amount but simply take a small percentage of the transaction. Many of the companies also charge a smaller amount for in-person swipes than transactions over the phone where there is no physical swiping of the card. Because of this try get the credit card in person instead of over the phone to save a little bit of money.

New and amazing smartphone programs continue to come out and you should use these programs to your advantage. There is no point in me listening the specific programs because by the time you read these some of them will be obsolete, and have been replaced with newer, cooler programs. The programs can help with billing, calendaring, accessing files, legal research, and pretty much any other need you will have. I believe that pretty much a whole practice can now be run from a smartphone.

One other form of technology that you must have is some sort of backup data storage. Many of the important documents you will have will be on your computer. Not only will your computer contain documents but it will also contain motions, filings, pleadings and many other things you do not want to lose. There are many options for data storage. There are traditional flash drives or external hard drives. There is nothing wrong with these devices but if you use them make sure you store them in a different place than your computer. If there is a fire at your office and your computer is next to your external hard drive, you will still lose everything.

Today, there are more data storage options that store information in off-site data centers. Many of these services are referred to as the "cloud" because your information is stored in a figurative cloud. I prefer off-site services because the data is always in a different place than your computer so they cannot both be destroyed at the same time. There are a number of companies that charge you a monthly or yearly amount to store your data. I prefer a free service called Dropbox. The program allows you store up to several gigs of data for free. If you want more storage you can add more for a fee. With the program, I can access files from any computer and from my smartphone. I can be sitting in court without my laptop and pull up any file that I have saved in my Dropbox. The bottom line is that one way or another, you must backup your data.

Along with a phone and a laptop you will need a decent scanner. A good scanner can save you an incredible amount of money and time. You will be able to save time as once a document is scanned it is much easier to manage that document. You will be able to access it not only from your computer but also from anywhere once you save it to your online storage program. Think of how much easier this can make your life. Say you are in court and opposing counsel or a judge needs some document. Without the document being scanned you would have to drive to your office, find the paper document, fax it and send it. If the document is already scanned you can pull it up on your phone and be done.

Scanning documents will also save you money. One way it will save you money is with storage costs. Instead of having to pay for physical space to store documents and discovery everything can be at your fingertips on your computer. Scanning documents and discovery will also save you money by freeing up your time, allowing you to work on other matters. To have a well-working scanned document system you will need to get and learn how to use Portable Document Folders, which are commonly referred to as PDFs.

PDF is a file format that makes storing legal documents and papers easy and cost-effective. While the basic version of PDF is free you will want to spend a little bit of money here and get the full program from Adobe Software. Adobe now offers a monthly subscription that gives you access to the full PDF program for several dollars a month. Once you have the full program you can do many cool things like turning PDF files into Word documents, as well as editing PDF documents. For a full explanation of the many, many benefits of learning how to use PDF, I recommend a book called *PDF Essentials for Lawyers* by Ernie Swenson. The book is available at his website at paperless-chase.com. The book not only lays out the many benefits of learning PDF but also teaches you how to use the program. Ernie Swenson is a good friend of mine and an expert on how PDF can save time and money for lawyers.

Another potentially useful technology is software designed for certain types of practices. I say potentially useful because you have to make sure the benefit outweighs the cost. If you will use the software, and it will make you money, then think about buying it. There are many different programs for attorneys. Some of the programs are designed to help with billing and trial prep. Some programs are designed for bankruptcy attorneys or immigration attorneys. I know both immigration attorneys and bankruptcy attorneys that would have a hard time functioning without their respective software.

At first you will probably not have the money for any software. Once you can afford the software, you must seriously ask yourself if you actually need it or is it just something cool that you kind of want. Remember that when you are starting out, managing your expenses will determine if your practice sinks or swims. Once you realize you need the software buy the best program that is available on the market. Talk to other attorneys in your field and they will tell you what program is best. I know that for bankruptcy attorneys there is one software program that is a lot better than its competition. Like most quality products this particular program costs more than the cheap knockoffs. One attorney told me they tried the cheaper program to save money. They told me the cheap program was so terrible that the money savings were not worth it.

The main lesson with technology is that it is always evolving and new and better products are always coming out. I am sure by the time you are reading this there will be new technology out that will make our lives easier and save us time. Learning how to use new technology can be difficult but it must be done. I know many attorneys that still use WordPerfect and never learned Word. One problem they are now having is that they are not able to file some documents with courts, as the documents have to be created in Word. The point is that attorneys must stay on top of new technologies.

When you start your own practice you will start getting calls from legal research providers. Westlaw and Lexis are the two biggest companies, but there are others. In general, I suggest you avoid subscribing to the services for several reasons. The first reason is cost. The services are incredibly expensive and generally not worth the price. With most of the services you can reduce the cost by paying for limited access. If you are practicing bankruptcy law in New York, you do not need access to maritime cases from Holland. The services will try to sign you to a multi-year contract, which can really add up over time.

The second reason I suggest avoiding "pay for use" services is because you can usually find places to do research for free. Most cities will have legal libraries that are free to use. When I started my practice, I would often do legal research at one of the downtown courthouses. I had free access to Westlaw and made good use of it. Another good place to find free Westlaw or another service is at your law school. Even if you have graduated most law schools will still let you use the library. Even if you are not close to your law school you may be able to use the local law school for research. Many law schools will allow in local attorneys to use their legal library.

If you are sharing an office with other attorneys, ask if you can pay them to use their online research provider. With the permission of the provider you may be able to get your own account for cheaper than it would be to buy your own account. Always remember that your biggest task is to find ways to save money.

Motions

As most of you know, a motion is a written request to the court. The motion can address something very simple like a Notice of Appearance. Motions can also address substantive matters like a Motion to Suppress or a Motion for a Directed Verdict. Motions, like all attorney work, should be done with a great degree of care and thought. You should never turn in a motion that you have not had someone read over for grammar and typo mistakes. You do not want a judge reading your motion and noticing that you confused "than" and "then" or don't know how to capitalize words correctly.

Depending on the type of practice you have, you may be writing many motions. For example, personal injury and criminal defense attorneys will write more motions than estate-planning attorneys. Some attorneys build an entire practice of motion writing. Attorneys who do post-conviction work or appeals work spend most of their time writing motions. Writing motions, like everything else, becomes easier with practice. When writing motions there is no substitution for experience, which comes with repetition. The first time I wrote a suppression motion it took me a lot more time than it takes me to write one now.

One of the keys to writing good motions is to remember that the wheel has already been invented. New attorneys must remember that there is nothing wrong with building off of someone else's motion. I will often talk to a fellow defense attorney and ask them if they have a motion that I can use. I can save myself a lot of time by building my motion off of someone else's compared to writing my own. In criminal defense, a lot of the same issues come up so why reinvent the wheel? If I have a probable cause issue that I know a friend of mine has a perfect motion for why write my own from scratch?

Never use someone else's motion without their permission as it is plagiarism and very unprofessional. When borrowing someone else's motion make sure you make all the necessary changes. I once got to watch a video of a judge screaming at a defense attorney who used someone else's motion, but forgot to make the necessary changes. The defense attorney forgot to change "she" to "he" and other made other obvious mistakes. Judges are OK with your motion building on someone else's, but they also want you to put the time in to make it correct.

Over time you will develop your own motion bank that will make your life easier. Every time you write a motion you should save it for future use. For example, I have a section in my own motion bank for Notice of Appearance Motions for different courts. I have one for each of the municipal courts, Justice of the Peace courts, and Superior Court. Every time I have to file a Notice of Appearance having the old motions saves me time, as I only have to change the dates and the defendant's name. The more motions you have in your motion bank the easier your life will be.

Expanding: Is Bigger Better?

At some point you will have to decide if you want to expand your practice. If you do expand you will also have to decide how big and how fast you want to grow. Many attorneys want to grow their practices because they want to make more money. Other attorneys want to make their practices bigger so the firm appears more prestigious. New attorneys must remember that there are perils to growing your practice. The first thing that new attorneys must think about is that a bigger firm doesn't mean a more profitable firm. A larger firm may take in more money but that doesn't mean it is netting more of a profit. Many firms learn this the hard way when it is too late. Consider the following hypothetical.

One attorney runs the Smith Law Firm. The attorney wants to expand her practice, so she hires two new paralegals and two associate attorneys. Ms. Smith goes out and spends a lot of money on advertising and the clients start coming and everyone is happy. All is good for a couple of months, but then the clients slow down. The advertising bills are still due, the salaries of the new employees must be paid and soon Ms. Smith is out of money. The bigger your practice, the more balls you are juggling. This happens all too often.

My financial planner recently told me about one of his other clients who is also a defense attorney. The attorney is pretty young and is trying to grow his practice. The attorney has an expensive office, two assistants and a paralegal. The young attorney has so much overhead that he has to take on more clients than he can handle just to cover the overhead. What will happen next is the clients he does have will be unhappy, as he is not able to spend enough time with them. The young attorney will be stuck in a vicious cycle just to stay afloat. With this example it is easy to see why many law practices fail.

Even if the clients don't stop coming, Ms. Smith has still increased her overhead by adding new employees. Ms. Smith may be grossing more profit, but when you subtract all the new expenses she may actually be making less money than she was before. Remember that just because you have more clients, it doesn't necessarily mean you are netting more of a profit.

The other thing that new attorneys must remember about expanding their practices is that the bigger the firm, the more problems you will have to deal with. When you have no employees, you don't have employee problems to deal with. When you have one employee you have one set of problems. When you have three employees you have three sets of problems. Instead of worrying about payroll, showing up late, insurance, workers comp, attitude issues and other problems for one person you now have to worry about those issues for three different people.

My point is not that expansion is bad. My point is that if you do decide to expand, first make sure it makes financial sense. Done correctly, expanding can net more of a profit. Also, make sure you are prepared to handle all the headaches that come with having an employee and that you absolutely need that employee. Right now I am busy enough that I could employ an assistant, but I choose not to. The reason I choose not to have an assistant is because I prefer to keep the money that I would be paying my assistant for myself.

If you do choose to expand, you need to decide what kind of vision you have for your growing practice. There are several different models that can be built. I have equated the type of firm with restaurants because it illustrates my point. It should go without saying that my descriptions generalize. There are excellent large firms and terrible small firms so size can be deceptive. As with everything in our profession, there are always exceptions. The first type of practice is the fast food model.

The fast food law firm model is high quantity, low quality. These types of firms depend on high-volume advertising. The firms are dependent on advertising as they get virtually no referrals because their clients are generally dissatisfied with the quality of work. The firms are usually large and can have anywhere from ten to thirty or more attorneys. In general, these firms are an embarrassment to the legal profession. Often these firms will advertise very low prices to get people in the door.

Once a potential client is in the door the firm uses a lot of high-pressure sales techniques. I have heard of some people taking potential client's ID and not giving it back until the potential client signs up. If you have ever been to a time-share sales presentation you get the idea. This type of practice is often attractive to attorneys because they can make a lot of money. The practice can be very profitable because of the large volume of clients that come to the firm. The large amount of money is made at the expense of reputation but some attorneys are OK with this trade-off. Unfortunately more and more of these firms are popping up in the fields of criminal defense, personal injury, bankruptcy and immigration.

The next type of law firm model is the national sit-down dinner restaurant model. The food is not great but not terrible. The restaurants have a lot of locations and the service is usually ok. Likewise, the service at these firms is often very middle-of-the-road. This type of firm does not rip off consumers but does very mediocre work. This model of practice is also often dependent on advertising. A firm using this model will have a number of attorneys and may expand or contract as needed. These types of firms can also be very profitable because of the large volume of clients.

Another type of law firm model is the small, expensive steakhouse model. These restaurants have excellent service and excellent food. These firms generally only have a few attorneys and do excellent work for a high price. Generally, experienced attorneys that have built up their reputation run these firms and now have potential clients come to them through referrals. These practices spend very little money on advertising and can be selective about the clients they want. If you do want employees or associate attorneys this is the type of practice you want to have. This model has the best of both worlds. You can still have other attorneys making money for you but the practice is small enough so you can make sure that the work being performed is up to your standards.

The last type of law firm is the hole-in-the-wall restaurant that has won every culinary award and has an eight-month waitlist. Solo attorneys usually run these practices. The attorneys that run these practices are often the best of the best and charge the most money. The attorneys running the practices are very selective about the clients they pick. The attorney is able to devote more attention to each client as they have fewer clients, but each client pays a lot. I cannot think of one of these attorneys that I know who has been in practice for less than 20 to 30 years.

Always remember that there is nothing wrong with wanting to keep your practice small. Don't forget that big doesn't automatically mean profitable, and vice-versa. For an excellent in-depth analysis of companies that have chosen to stay small I recommend the book *Small Giants: Companies That Choose to Be Great Instead of Big* by Bo Burlingham. The book looks at a number of companies that have made the choice to not grow to be as big as possible. The companies, for various reasons, have decided that the best way for them to operate is to limit their size. The lessons in the book are important for lawyers with their own practice because it shows that bigger is not always better.

Hiring Staff

When you are ready to hire an employee, there are a number of factors you must think about. One of the first things you need to think about is how much you will pay your new employee. Obviously the more you pay, the more experienced and qualified candidates you will get. If you are looking for a paralegal/assistant and you are offering to pay minimum wage, you will get minimum wage applicants. While this is generally the rule it is not always true. You may be able to find an excellent employee that is willing to accept a lower wage. Again, this is the exception to the rule and generally you will get what you pay for. When deciding how much to pay a new employee, talk to other attorneys and ask what they are paying. Once you know what other attorneys are paying their staff, you will have a better idea what to pay yours.

The next factor you must consider is what type of personality do you want your new employee to have. Do you want someone who is very talkative or quiet? Someone who is introverted or outgoing? If you are very outgoing you may not want an employee who is the same way. The point is that you must think about the traits you want in an employee before you hire someone. Like every part of running a practice, deciding on the type of employee you want takes preparation and planning. Once you know how much you will be paying and what traits you want in an employee you will have to conduct interviews.

Interviews are a great way to learn about someone but remember that they are like first dates. The person you are interviewing is putting on a show for you and trying to impress you. Interviewing someone is not enough. You must get references. If someone doesn't have references this is a red flag. Once you hire someone you must immediately be clear with him or her what your expectations are. If you want your employees dressed a certain way or to mark files a certain way you must tell them this. If you expect your employee to be on time and not five minutes late every day this must also be made clear to them. The more you communicate your expectations, the better the chances that the employee will do what you ask.

Also consider that that while you want an employee you get along with, it is equally important that the employee can get along with you. When speaking with potential employees make sure they understand your personality, your work demands, and how you run your practice. Be honest about what you are and are not when interviewing people. For example, if you are brash and loud do not hide this. Conversely, if you are incredibly soft-spoken don't try to be loud during the interview. The more open you are initially, the better things will go in the long run. If you don't reveal what you are actually like until the employee starts working for you it could be too late.

Management Skills

There are a million management books and I do not pretend or claim to be an expert on management. My whole career I have worked to set up my practice so I have to manage as few people as possible. I didn't go to law school to end up in a human relations job. I will say the following about management.

I am a big fan of Warren Buffet. I am a fan of his not only because he has managed to build his own empire, but also because of how he manages his empire. There are several Warren Buffet rules that you can apply to your own law office and your own management. The rules are simple but valuable. The first rule is think long term. When you are hiring a staff person ask if they will be a good long-term fit for your practice. When training a new employee take a long-term approach and teach them that it is more important that they do things the right way and not the fast way. The second rule is being patient. When training a new employee be patient with them. You breathing down the neck of your new employee is not going to make them learn any faster. Patience is not only important for training employees but for your practice in general. Patience is needed in everything from dealing with employees to expectations of growth for the whole practice.

The third rule is to avoid micromanaging. The reason you have employees is to help you make more money and to help you manage your time. If your employee is training well there is no reason to micromanage them. If they are poorly trained that is your fault and you need to spend more time on training them. Micromanaging also has the effect of eroding the confidence of the employee. If you are constantly standing over their shoulder or doing their work for them obviously this will have an effect on the employee.

The fourth rule, and maybe the most valuable, is to avoid doing what everyone else is doing. Remember that just because everyone is doing something one way doesn't automatically mean that is the best way. One of the things that makes Warren Buffet so unique is that he will go against the grain when he thinks it is the right thing to do. There have been countless times when most investors were running from a stock or a company while Buffet was buying up the stock as fast as he could. Don't be afraid to do something different if you think it will work better. For example, if everyone in your law building is underpaying his or her legal assistants and you are overpaying yours, it doesn't mean you are wrong. A personal example is that I got a work cell phone because it was saving me money over a traditional work phone. Most attorneys still had traditional landlines because that was the norm.

The last Warren Buffet rule is to value simplicity. There are many different ways to value simplicity. Simplicity can be seen in the type of law you are doing. Doing seven types of law is not valuing simplicity as you have to stay up to date on seven different areas of law. Having a huge expensive office that you do not need is not valuing simplicity as you are spending more money than you needed to. With every area of your practice you should be asking yourself if there is a simpler, more efficient way to do things.

The last important tip I can give on management is that your firm and your employees will take on the attitude you set. If you are positive, honest, and hardworking your employees will be also. If you cut corners, are dishonest, and unethical your employees will be too. I see this in action a lot with judges and their staff. If a judge is cranky and unpleasant their staff will usually be the same. Conversely, if the judge is pleasant and welcoming their staff will be too.

Using Experts

Pretty much any experienced attorney will tell you that they use experts. A common mistake new attorneys make is not using experts enough. Experienced attorneys know that a good expert will more than pay for themselves. An experienced attorney also knows that a good expert can give insight that the attorney may have missed or simply did not know about. A good expert will be useful not only during trial but also before trial, and sometimes even before a case is filed.

Depending on the field of law you are in different experts will be commonly used. For criminal defense attorneys such as myself there are a number of experts that are commonly used. Experts in the areas of drugs, ballistics, psychiatry, and many other areas are used. Any personal injury attorney will have expert doctors that they consult with and use for trial. Obviously medical malpractice attorneys will also have doctors that they use. I currently do a lot of DUI defense work and use an expert who is a scientist who specializes in blood alcohol concentration and how alcohol affects the body. It is rare that I have done a DUI trial and not used this particular expert.

One reason that many new attorneys do not use experts as much as they should is because a good expert is not cheap. The expert I use charges about $600 to testify and bills hourly on top of the $600 flat fee. A good expert is expensive for several reasons. The first reason is that a good expert will have a lot of experience in the field they are testifying on and know that their expertise is valuable. Another reason is that often there are not many experts in a narrow field so the ones that are available know they can charge more. With experts you get what you pay for. You can go out and get a cheap expert but the cheapness will show. A bad expert will be bad at spotting issues, bad at testifying and could possibly hurt your case more than they help.

When trying to decide if you want or need an expert remember that experts can come from a wide variety of people. Most attorneys only think of doctors and scientists but you need to think more broadly. For example, I have used former police officers as experts in cases where I questioned if the police did something wrong. Remember almost anyone can be an expert under the Rules of Evidence. Don't be afraid to be creative when trying to decide who can be an expert witness for your side. You owe it to your client to do everything you can to help them and using good experts is part of that responsibility.

The last thing to remember with experts is who is going to pay for them. Are you paying the expert or is the client? If the client is paying the expert they obviously must be told this. I can't go to a client who has hired me for several thousand dollars and then tell them I need another thousand dollars for an expert. I have a brief statement in my fee agreement that the client will be responsible for any experts that are needed. If the client cannot afford the expert at least I have told the client that the expert was available. Some attorneys will charge more for a case when they know an expert will be needed. For example if they are charging two thousand dollars and the expert's cost will be five hundred dollars they will charge the client $2,500 and pay the expert themselves. The bottom line is that from the beginning of the case you must be clear with the client as to who will be responsible for paying the expert.

Outsourcing

One of the new developments in solo practice in the last couple of years is the idea of outsourcing. Outsourcing used to be only an option for large and midsize firms but today it is available to solo attorneys and small firms. Outsourcing can be defined in different ways but for our purposes outsourcing is any time you get someone outside of your firm to do work for you. The outsourced work can be anything from online research to motion drafting to editing documents.

There are several big advantages to outsourcing some of your legal work. The biggest benefit is cost. If you are using an overseas company for your outsourcing you might pay a fraction of the cost that you would pay for non-outsourced work. For example, an Indian company might charge you $100 to research an issue while a local paralegal might charge $1000 for the same work.

Another potential benefit of outsourcing has to do with time differences. If you are using a company located in Asia for your outsourcing needs, their nighttime is daytime here in the United States. What this means is that if you give the company a project in the evening it can often be ready in the morning. While you are sleeping someone is doing your work for you.

One potential downside of outsourcing for law firms is that you don't always know if you will be receiving quality legal work. If you are using a company or a person for the first time, how do you know they are competent and will do what you ask for? One employee of an outsourcing company could do the best legal research you have ever seen while another employee at the same company could be totally useless.

One way to increase your odds of getting high-quality work is to do your research. Read reviews of the company you are thinking about hiring online. Ask the company for referrals and names of other lawyers they have done work for. Actually talk to the people they give you and ask a lot of questions. If a company is not willing to give you references this is an obvious red flag. If you prefer not to go overseas with your legal work there are plenty of services and companies in the United States that offer the same services.

For an excellent discussion on outsourcing check out Tim Ferris' excellent book called *The Four Hour Work Week*. The book addresses many of the hesitations people have when considering outsourcing some of their needs. The book also brings up many excellent questions to ask when interviewing potential outsourcing companies that you may be thinking of hiring. I personally have learned a lot about outsourcing from the book. When using outsourcing, like with everything, there is some trial and error so you will have to play around with it and give it some time.

Continuing Legal Education

All lawyers are required to participate in a certain number of continuing legal education ("CLE") hours. Every state has different requirements and you must become familiar with your own state and your local rules. Arizona, for example, requires lawyers to obtain 15 CLE hours every year. Out of those 15, three must deal with ethics.

One thing to watch out for with CLE requirements is that different states have different rules on how many CLE hours you can carry over from one year to the next. One state might allow five hours while a different state might not allow any. Obviously this can make a big difference because if you are planning on carrying over hours and this is not allowed in your state you will have a problem on your hands.

There are many different ways to earn CLE hours. Before the Internet CLE classes were either offered in person or on audio or videotapes. Today there are many companies that offer online CLE classes. There is nothing wrong with online CLE classes but if you are doing them through a private company make sure your state bar accredits the CLE so you get credit for the CLE. Most CLE companies are reputable and accredit their CLE classes, but there are shady CLE companies out there.

There are also many CLE opportunities at conferences. There are state bar conferences held by the state bar once or twice a year. There are also specialty law conferences that focus on specific areas of law. For example, there are a number of conferences that focus on criminal law. More specifically, there are seminars that focus exclusively on DUI law. As with everything not all seminars are equally well organized or have the best content. Before signing up for a conference talk to other lawyers to find out what conferences are worth attending.

While conferences will be more expensive than online CLE classes there are several advantages to conferences. One advantage is the opportunity for networking. If you are at a conference there may be hundreds of other lawyers that you can network with and gain potential mentors and sources of information. If you are a new lawyer a conference can be a goldmine for networking.

Another potential advantage of attending a conference is that you can immerse yourself in the material for several days. I always enjoy conferences because I feel like I can really get into the material and spend time digesting what I have learned. While there are advantages to earning CLE credits through conferences there is one big downside, and that is cost. Good conferences are not cheap. With conferences you usually get what you pay for. If you attend a two-day conference that costs $100, chances are it will not be a great conference.

When you are just starting out the cost of CLE classes should be a large consideration. Don't forget to look for free CLE classes. When I was a new attorney and had no money and could not afford criminal law CLE classes I would attend CLE classes on different areas of the law. I would still learn something and get free CLE credit. Check with your state bar and other local legal organizations to find out about low-cost, or free, CLE opportunities.

Another great way to save on CLE costs is to put on your own CLE. Different states have different rules, but in Arizona if you put on a CLE presentation you can count some of the preparation time to your CLE hours. For example, if you spend an hour preparing a CLE presentation you are giving then you can count that one hour towards your required amount of CLE for that year. When you are a new lawyer finding people that will want you to present a CLE will be difficult but not impossible. As always, hustle until you succeed.

Chapter 11

What No One Told You in Law School (But Should Have)

A Lot More Gray in Real Life

One of the major differences between being in law school and actually practicing is the amount of gray. In law school, there is a lot more black and white, and right and wrong. When you begin to practice you see that answers are rarely clear-cut. In law school there is always a right answer. Whether it is in class on an exam or a quiz, most of the time the professor will say there is a correct answer. If it's in contracts class the professor will say if a contract has been formed. If the question is in torts the professor will tell you if an intentional tort has been committed. Obviously there are gray areas in law school but things are a lot grayer in actual practice.

Just one example of how things are less black and white in actual practice is how judges rule on motions and evidentiary issues. When you are in law school, the judge in a casebook always makes the right decision. If something is not admissible under the rules of evidence the judge makes the right call. If a search violated the Fourth Amendment the judge suppresses the evidence. In real practice, judges do not always make the right call. Sometimes the judge makes the wrong call because they don't understand the law or sometimes they do not like you or the defendant. In real life judges are people and they make mistakes. Talk to any practicing attorney and they will tell you stories of judges making mistakes. This is not to say that judges normally get things wrong, because that would not be fair. Judges try to do a good job and get most things correct, but not always.

There Is No Safety Net

When you are a practicing attorney, there is no safety net. If you make a serious mistake you can be sued, suspended, or even disbarred. I don't say this to scare new attorneys, but to make you aware of a harsh reality. When you are in law school, even if you fail a class, you can retake it. In practice you are

125

usually not given a chance to fix a mistake. Every month the Arizona State Bar publishes a list of the attorneys that have been suspended or disbarred and the length of the list always shocks me.

In law school there is much more of a support system than in real practice. In law school there are guidance counselors, tutors, deans and other people that can help. In practice, attorneys are often on their own. As long as new attorneys understand this at the beginning, they can plan accordingly. Attorneys must go out and find people to help them and mentor them. New attorneys should understand that they must build their own support system where they can turn for guidance.

When you are a practicing attorney you must understand that your law license is your livelihood. If you have a law practice and you get suspended you cannot practice law. How will you feed your family, pay your mortgage, and stay afloat? I protect my law license because I understand that license is how I make a living.

Clients Generally Do Not Care Where You Went to School

In law school, there is a lot of focus on law school rankings and what tier your school is. In general clients don't care about where you went to school. Clients care about results and if you can help them. Also where you went to law school will not dictate your success or failure in the legal profession. If you went to a super prestigious law school this does not guarantee success. If you went to the lowest-ranked law school in the country you can still become a world-class attorney. What will dictate your success or failure is your ability to work hard and learn, not where you went to school. In four years of practice I have had exactly one defendant ask me where I went to law school. The defendant was court appointed and homeless. New attorneys that did not go to prestigious top-tier law schools must remember that they can be just as competent as any famous law school attorney.

People in the legal community know which attorneys are competent and which are not. When I talk to my attorney friends none of us have ever said: "She is a wildly incompetent attorney but she went to a super good, big name law school so she is still a good attorney." I know plenty of terrible attorneys that went to big name law schools. I also know some excellent attorneys that went to fourth-tier law schools.

When a client walks into your office they may be impressed by your law school but they will be a lot more impressed by your reputation and your competence. Every criminal defense client would rather have an attorney that went to a no-name law school but got their buddy out of prison than a Harvard grad that doesn't know where the criminal court is. I really believe even corporate clients at big prestigious law firms would rather have a competent attorney than a weak attorney who went to a prestigious law school. Do not let where you went to school dictate your mindset.

Likable > Knowledgeable

If you asked most law students if it is more important for an attorney to be likeable or knowledge, they will say knowledgeable. If you ask most practicing attorneys, they will tell you the opposite. Obviously, the best attorneys are likable and knowledgeable, but many attorneys are one and not the other. An attorney that is knowledgeable but not likeable will have a hard time making a living. They will have a hard time making a living because they will have a hard time getting clients. They will also have a hard time dealing with other attorneys and judges.

An attorney that is likable only will probably have a more profitable career than a knowledgeable, non-likable attorney. Clients want to like their attorneys. I have seen many criminal defense attorneys build profitable practices while knowing very little of the law. The reason these attorneys can build profitable practices is because they are able to get clients and the clients refer other clients to them because they like them. I also know attorneys that are incredibly knowledgeable on the law but can hardly make a living as no one wants to hire them. My point is not to tell people that knowledge is not important, because it is. My point is that new attorneys must understand that they must be likeable not only for clients, but for other attorneys and judges.

A Frightening Number of Incompetent Attorneys

There are an amazing number of incompetent attorneys. Some are lazy, some have substance abuse issues, some are burned-out, and some were never very good attorneys to start with. There are incompetent people in every profession, and attorneys are no different. Just as there are bad plumbers, nurses, roofers, or gardeners, there are bad attorneys. New attorneys need to know that there are bad attorneys for several reasons. The problem with an incompetent attorney is the great amount of damage they can do. An incompetent attorney can get an innocent person sent to prison, cost someone his or her life savings or, at the least, hurt the reputation of the legal profession.

The first reason is that no matter what field of law you are in you will have to deal with bad attorneys. If you are a prosecutor you will have to deal with incompetent defense attorneys. If you are a civil attorney you will have to deal with incompetent opposing counsel. New attorneys must be prepared for the reality that they will deal with attorneys that have no idea what they are talking about. If you are a new attorney and your opposing counsel is incompetent, the sooner you realize that the better off you will be. A new attorney must never assume that just because someone is an attorney they are automatically competent.

The second reason is that new attorneys must understand that it is up to them to repair the reputational harm of attorneys caused by incompetent attorneys. New attorneys must always remember that they are representatives of a profession and must do everything in their power to present that profession in the best light possible. Every time a new attorney is competent and does the right thing this helps the reputation of attorneys.

There is not only an amazing number of incompetent attorneys but there is an amazing amount of incompetence everywhere. From judges to support staff, there are a lot of people who are not good at their jobs. Some of this is from laziness, and some is from a lack of training. I have had to deal with bailiffs and clerks in many different courts that have made all kinds of mistakes. I have had clerks set trials on holidays, forget to give defendants their paper work, and lose entire court files. Again, the legal profession is no different than any profession in this regard.

Managing Student Loans

There are some things you can do to prepare for repayment of your loans while you are still in law school. One of the keys to dealing with lenders is to be proactive. If your loans go into default, you will have less options than if you deal with them sooner.

One way to be proactive is to contact your providers and ask them about different repayment programs. You will need to do your homework and learn about the different programs. With some of the programs the interest is paused while with others the interest continues to accrue but you do not have to make regular payments. If your loans are with different providers, you may want to look into consolidating your loans. If your loans are consolidated you may be able to get a better interest rate. Another advantage of consolidation is that if your loans are all in one place it is easier to know what is going on with them.

Most of your loans will have some kind of grace period after you graduate. Depending on the type of loan and lender the period can be from six months to a year. Get all the details from the lender and take full advantage of any grace periods that are offered. Once you do have to pay back the loans ask about what type of income-based repayment options are offered. Income-based repayment programs are exactly what they sound like. Every year you submit financial documents to your lender and they work out a new payment amount. The big advantage of the income-based program is that your monthly payments will be a lot lower than the traditional repayment plan.

I can't stress how important it is that you stay on top of your student loans. The loan provider companies are like the Motor Vehicle Department. If they can screw something up they will. While working on this section I thought I should check on my income-based repayment application that I have to resubmit every year. After twenty minutes on hold I found out that Sallie Mae has processed my application too early (I didn't know that could be done). Long story short, I straightened everything out. If I had not called them today my income-based repayment program would have been messed up for the whole year and it would have cost me a lot of money and a lot of stress.

There is no worse feeling than when your lenders are calling you and telling you owe more money than you have. I remember the first time I got a call from a lender telling me they wanted more money than I had and how it felt. It is not a good feeling. I have had many friends that were not able to make their payments because they failed to plan. Ideally you should start planning on how you will manage your loans before you graduate. Burying your head in the sand and avoiding the issue will not help. The longer you put off making arrangements to pay the worse off you will be. No one hates dealing with lenders more than I do, but it is simply something that must be done. You must stay on top of your loans.

Many Attorneys Never Make a Lot of Money

There are several reasons why there is a perception that all attorneys are rich. One cause of this is that there are some attorneys that make huge amounts of money. There are partners at huge firms that make insane amounts of money. Another reason I think the perception exists is that many attorneys like to pretend they have a lot of money. The last reason I think that the perception exists is popular media. Films like *The Firm* show law school graduates being offered huge paychecks upon graduation. The reality is often very different for attorneys.

A huge number of attorneys live paycheck to paycheck. No doubt some of this is because of their own poor planning. As discussed if you do not manage your money you will have no money. Many attorneys are not bad with money but simply do not earn a lot. Some attorneys do not earn very much because they work for the government. Many government agencies currently have pay increase freezes due to budget cuts. What this means for attorneys working in those offices is that they cannot get a pay increase even if they deserve it.

Many private attorneys don't make a lot of money for a different reason. As discussed there are more and more attorneys competing for the same clients. Attracting private clients may mean spending a lot of advertising. Many private attorneys simply do not have the money to advertise. Some private attorneys are able to rely on referrals for clients but not all can. Many clients will speak to four or five attorneys before picking one. This tells me that there is a lot more supply than demand. It is important that new attorneys understand that many attorneys never make a lot of money.

Importance of Momentum

I first started thinking about momentum about six months ago. I had applied for the third time for a contract that was incredibly lucrative and after two years of trying had finally gotten the position. About two weeks later I was awarded another lucrative contract that I had applied for several months before. At about the same time I had several private clients hire me for large cases. It seemed to me that success was breeding more success. At the time I was thinking that when I was starting my practice I would have killed for one contract or one private client and now within weeks of each other I was getting both.

I believe that in any business that success leads to more success. Many people describe this as the snowball effect. As the snowball gains speed it gains size which makes it gain even more speed. When you are starting your practice or your career your job is to get the snowball rolling. The bigger the snowball gets the faster it goes. Remember to be patient. My practice putted along for four years before it took off. Talk to virtually any business owner and they will tell you that things were very slow at first and that it took a lot of time and hard work to get things going. Think of those strong man competitions where huge objects are pulled. The hardest part is the beginning as the object to be pulled is standing still — getting it rolling is the hardest part. Once the object is moving our friend momentum does a lot of the work.

Haters Hating

Urban Dictionary describes hating as jealousy and anger rolled up in one.[1] In every profession there are haters; the legal profession is no different. When

---

1. http://www.urbandictionary.com/define.php?term=hating

attorneys who are not happy with how their own careers are going see an attorney doing well they will hate. Think back to high school when one student did well on every exam and the students that did poorly made fun of the student who spent all his or her time studying. I think the legal profession may have more jealousy in it due to the fact that many lawyers are competitive by nature. The more competitive a person is the more they want to succeed.

I am always amazed how much I hear and see attorneys hating on other attorneys who are doing well. The attorneys doing the hating rarely look inward and ask themselves, Why am I not as successful as I want to be? What they should do is look at what the successful attorney is doing that they are not. This would actually be helpful and productive. An even more useful course of action would be to go to the attorney and to ask to learn from them. Ask them how they are getting clients or managing their practice. What lawyers that are haters chose to do is to hate on the attorney they are jealous of. This is not constructive or useful but they do it anyway. The hating attorney will say the other attorney is simply lucky or dishonest or make up other things to bring down the other attorneys.

The lesson for the new attorney is two-fold. First, don't be a hater. Hating on other attorneys does not help you and fills your head with negative energy. Negative energy creates more negative energy. Second, if someone hates on you ignore that person. Remember that often hating comes down to jealousy and someone's own issues with themselves and not actually with you. Focus on yourself and not on the person who is hating on you. I have noticed the more successful I have become the more people hate on me behind my back. I chose not to focus on these people, as focusing on them would not help anything.

Developing People Skills/Reading People

When I was thinking about this section I thought of doing two different sections but then decided that the sections belong together. The reason the two sections belong together is because the better your people skills are the better you will be at reading people. Having strong people skills is absolutely essential in having your own practice. I would even go so far as to say it is virtually impossible to succeed long-term in having your own practice without people skills.

First, what do I mean by people skills? People skills are a combination of skills that include being able to talk to people, listening, gaining someone's trust, and being likeable. People skills are no different than any other skill and take practice. The more you deal with people, the better your people skills will get. Obviously some people have better people skills than others. If you do not have strong people skills this will be something you will need to work on.

It is crucial that young attorneys understand the importance of people skills. How are you going to get clients to hire you if you can't talk to them or if they do not like you? A client is never going to hire an attorney if they do not like them. I know several attorneys who are very good attorneys but severely lack people skills. These attorneys cannot figure out why no one will hire them despite the fact they are very knowledgeable and skilled. The reason these attorneys can't get clients to hire them is because they lack people skills. People skills do not mean you like all your clients, far from it. I have many clients that I don't like but I still have to have them like me or they will not hire me. Just as developing people skills takes practice, reading people also takes practice.

Reading people is more art than science. It is part body language, part character, and part guessing. Being able to read people is an incredibly valuable skill for attorneys for several reasons. First, if you are able to read people you will be better at screening out problem clients. A problem client is someone who hires you and later on you wish they had hired someone else, as they are more trouble than they are worth. Second, reading people is valuable as you are better able to deal with not only your own clients but also opposing counsel, witnesses, and judges.

At this point I have been in practice long enough that I can get an excellent read on a new client before even talking to them. I can look at someone's facial expressions, body language, posture, and other signs and guess with amazing accuracy how things will go once we start talking. There are a million examples of how this is a useful skill for attorneys. I can't tell you how many times I have been able to come up with a successful approach to cross-examine a witness just from getting a read on them while they are on the stand.

Knowing How to Sell Yourself

A large part of running your own practice has to do with sales. A lot of attorneys think that running their own practice is only about practicing law but this is simply not true. In order to have a practice you have to have clients and to have clients you have to convince clients to hire you. It doesn't matter if you are the greatest attorney in the world if you can't get someone to hire you.

If you are in the printer business you have to convince people to buy your printers. If you are in the drug industry you have to convince your clients that your drugs are better than the drugs from the guy down the street. For attorneys there is no product that we are selling. As an attorney you are selling yourself and your services. If you are a bad drug dealer but you have awesome drugs you will still have customers. If you are not good at selling yourself as an attorney you will go out of business, as you are the product. This is worth repeating: YOU ARE THE PRODUCT.

As there are more and more attorneys competing for the same clients it is more important than ever to be able to sell yourself. If you want a client and that client has talked to four other attorneys, why should the client hire you and not the other attorneys? The bigger the market you are in the more attorneys will be competing over the same clients. If you are in a small market you still have to know how to sell. If in a large city there are 200 attorneys competing over 2,000,000 million clients the problem is different in a small market. There may be 2 attorneys but there are only 2,000 potential clients. The point is no matter the size of the market you must be able to sell yourself.

One of the more successful attorneys I know used to be a vice-president in a software company. A huge part of her job was selling. She had to sell clients and investors on her products. Today she is successful because she is a very skilled attorney but also because she knows how to sell.

I do not come from a sales background so when I started my own practice I did not know how to sell myself. To be good at sales you have to be a little pushy and persistent and I was not good at this right away. When I say a little pushy I do not mean be like a used-car salesman. What I mean is that you cannot take no for an answer. You have to convince a potential client to become an actual client. The art of selling is outside the scope of this book but I can tell you that being good at sales and selling yourself, like everything else, takes practice.

If you are not good at sales or do not come from a sales background there are steps you can take to get better. Find an attorney who is good at sales and ask to shadow them. You will be amazed how much you learn. If you can't find an attorney to mentor you, there are great books on learning how to sell. Another good idea is to attend a seminar on the art of selling. Remember, the more you invest in your skills the greater the payoff will be.

There Are Too Many Attorneys

Sorry to be the bearer of bad news. The legal market is oversaturated with attorneys. I know this to be the case in Phoenix and by all indications it is true in every city. I tell you this not to bum you out and make you feel bad about the huge investment of time and energy you made in getting your law degree. I tell you this so you can do something about it.

One of the things you can do to help your odds has to do with the area of law you practice. A defense attorney will generally have harder time finding work than a patent attorney. A family law attorney will have harder time finding work than a tax attorney. The reason is that there is more competition. While there are more clients seeking the help of family or criminal law attorneys there are also a lot more defense and family attorneys. Remember that there are a million different fields of law and some are more oversaturated than others. Also remember that every market is different. For example, there will be more need for patent attorneys in San Francisco than there will be in North Dakota. Conversely, there will be more need for attorneys that specialize in beef subsidies in North Dakota than there will in San Francisco. These are all things you need to think about when deciding what area of law to focus on and where you want your practice to be located.

One other thing you can do to help your odds is to be at the right place at the right time. The best way to find out about opportunities is to be around people in the know. It is very unlikely that you will hear about an opening for a contract that you want if you are sitting at home. If you want a contact in Court A you have to spend time in Court A. As I have mentioned before you have to know the decision makers, and the best way to get to know the decision makers is to be in the same place as them. Every court I have ever gotten a contract in was one I had spent a lot of time in and had gotten to know the people. Never forget that people want to hire people they know and like.

Be Careful Who You Talk To

"Loose Lips Sink Ships"
— United States World War II Poster

Attorneys love to complain about other attorneys and about judges to each other. There is nothing wrong with complaining about someone you do not like or someone that annoys you. There are plenty of judges and attorneys that I do not like. I am not telling you not to complain. I am telling you to be careful with whom you share your thoughts. Here is a typical example that happens all too often. Attorney A goes to Attorney B and says I hate Attorney C. Attorney A doesn't know that Attorney B and Attorney C are best friends. You would be amazed how often variations of the above example happen. Recently a friend of mine was complaining to a friend of hers about a prosecutor. What my friend didn't know realize was that the friend and prosecutor grew up friends and were very close. There are two ways to not get yourself into trouble.

The first way is the easiest and it involves not saying anything bad about anyone. The second approach is more realistic. Develop a close circle of people that you trust and share things with them. I have a group of five or six attorneys that I can share things with in confidence. I can share with this group of friends and not have to worry about who will find out about my conversation. If you talk about everyone to everyone sooner or later you will get yourself in trouble.

Not All Comparable Work Pays Comparably Well

Just because two people do essentially the same work does not mean they are paid the same. One difference can be related to geographic area. As I have mentioned, I have a friend who works for a government agency in the Midwest. If he worked for the same type of agency in Arizona he would be paid about $20,000 dollars more per year. While geographic areas can make a difference in pay, similar jobs in the same location can also pay very differently.

One example of difference in pay is contract work. For example, I have two city contracts to represent indigent defendants charged with criminal offenses. The cities that give the contracts do not have full-time public defenders so they pay attorneys like me to take cases. My job duties in the two contracts are virtually identical. I get assigned defendants and handle their criminal matters. The big difference is that one of the contracts pays almost four times as much. Same type of work, same location, huge pay difference. Many of my fellow attorneys that only have the lower-paying contract have no idea that there is another contract that pays four times as much.

The reason for the discrepancy is that every city, county and state has its own budget and makes its own decisions how much to pay and to whom. The locations where I have the two contracts are only minutes apart but pay very differently. I have also heard of county contracts ranging a lot in pay even though the counties can be right next to each other.

It is obvious that higher paying work is better than lower paying work. The key to finding the higher paying positions is networking. The way I found that there was a contract that paid so much was because I knew some of the attorneys that already had the higher-paying contract. If I had not been friends with attorneys that had the contract I would have never known, never applied, and never gotten the higher paying contract. The idea of similar work paying very differently goes beyond contracts and government positions.

I have been in court with two different DUI attorneys and from talking to them I learned that one was making twice as much as the other, even though their clients were charged with the exact same crime. The reason one attorney was able to charge twice is much is multi-faceted, but it ultimately comes down to the fact that his client was willing to pay. I don't know if the attorney who was charging half as much never asked for more money or asked and was turned down. The bottom line is that two attorneys were doing the same work but one was making twice the money. Never forget that your practice is a business and the goal of a business is to make money.

Building Relationships Takes Time

When I started my practice there was this one attorney that would never say hi to me. Every time I saw him I said hello or hi and every time he ignored me. When I spoke to other attorneys about him they always said they didn't know much about him and that they didn't know why he was ignoring me. The attorney that was ignoring me was in his sixties and was an institution of the court and had been around longer than the building. He ignored me for the better part of two years. At some point the strangest thing happened. He started talking to me and he never stopped. Every time I see him he talks my ear off and couldn't be nicer.

I figured out that he was the type of person that took a long time to warm up to someone. This had not occurred me because that is not my personality. I will talk to anyone at any time and don't need time to warm up to people. This attorney was different, and once he felt comfortable around me his whole demeanor and personality changed. Now I consider him a friend but getting to that point took years. I have met several other attorneys that were also initially not very friendly but warmed up to me over time. Remember that people are cautious around new people. Don't expect to build relationships overnight.

Think of one of your best friends and how long it took you before you considered them your best friend. Remember this when dealing with attorneys, support staff, judges, and anyone else you deal with professionally. The fact that building trust takes time is especially important to remember when it comes to clients.

I have lost track of how many times clients have warmed up to me over time. Many clients did not trust me at first but when they realized that I was on their side and trying to help them their personality and disposition toward me changed. Don't expect that after you spend five minutes with a client they will trust you. A client may not trust you the second or third time you meet them but eventually if you do a good job they will trust you. That being said, some clients will never trust you. As long as you have done quality work for them and treated them with respect there is nothing you can do.

Make Yourself Irreplaceable

One of the best pieces of advice that I can give you is that you have to find ways to make yourself irreplaceable to the people that pay you. These people might be your private clients or courts where you have contracts. The more dependent the people paying you are on you, the more irreplaceable you will become. If you are handling a small case for a client they can imagine firing you or hiring a different lawyer for their next case. If you are handling a number of matters for that same client it will be harder for that client to hire someone else for their next case. In other words, the more the person needs the more job security you will have.

There are many examples of how lawyers can make themselves irreplaceable. I have a lawyer friend who works as city prosecutor for a small town in Arizona. He is the only prosecutor and because he is the only one that can do that job in that court he is irreplaceable to that court. The court knows that if they wanted to replace him it would be a huge inconvenience to them. If there were 30 prosecutors in that court and they wanted to get rid of my friend he would be very replaceable.

Another example is a different lawyer friend of mine who does court-appointed work. One of the courts he works for has four individual courtrooms and there are two contract public defenders per courtroom. This means there are eight public defenders total. My friend is the assigned public defender in three different courtrooms. In other words, my friend is 3/8 of the public defenders in that court. My friend is very much irreplaceable. If the court wanted to replace almost half of their PD staff it would be a huge inconvenience to the court. If my friend were only assigned in one courtroom, he would be easier to replace as the court would have to replace only 1/8 of their public defenders.

The bottom line is that you need to be constantly thinking of how you can make yourself more irreplaceable. Being irreplaceable will give you more job security and job security will give you greater financial security.

Chapter 12

Quality of Life Issues

"The job will not save you."
— Lester Freamon, *The Wire*

As I have stated before, there are many unhappy attorneys. When you are in law school this is not something you are told but it is something that you need to know. One source of attorneys not being as happy as they want to be is the idea that they are not making enough money. Like everything, there is a positive and a negative way to look at your income.

You will only be as happy as your expectations. In other words, happiness is relative. If you expect to make millions and you make less, then you will not be happy. The idea works both ways. If you expect to make $40,000 and you make $50,000 you will be thrilled. Guess how much I made in my first year of practice? I made barely over $25,000 for the year. I didn't make a lot but I was thrilled. I had made more than zero and I made enough to pay the bills and go forward to my second year. If I had started my practice thinking that if I made less than $30,000 I would be disappointed and angry, that's exactly what would have happened. How much money you make has to be seen in perspective

Perspective is the key to many things in life. One of my favorite TV shows is *Deadliest Journeys*. The show follows people around the world with dangerous jobs. One episode features sulfur miners in Indonesia. The miners walk up the side of a volcano carrying hundreds of pounds of sulfur on their back. The miners go up the side of the volcano in flip-flops because those are the only shoes they can afford. Most of the miners die around forty years of age from breathing the fumes.

Earlier I said I made *only* $25,000 my first year. The sulfur miners will not make $25,000 in their entire lives. This is perspective. A large part of your happiness or unhappiness in the legal profession will depend on your outlook. If you think about how fortunate you are to not have to be a sulfur miner in Indonesia you will be happier. If you think about how you are not making as much as another attorney you will be less happy. Simple but true. Worrying about money is one source of attorney unhappiness. Not appreciating their jobs is another source of unhappiness.

Many attorneys would be happier if they remembered how lucky they are to be attorneys. Remember what percentage of the world would love to do what attorneys get to do. How many people wish they had a job where they get to dress up, sit in an air-conditioned office, and give advice to people. This is one way to look at what attorneys do. This is mostly my approach, and it helps me to keep things in perspective. Other attorneys have a different outlook. They complain about not making enough money, about hating their clients, about other things they do not like and they end up unhappy. You will have to decide what your outlook is. Your outlook will have a huge effect on how happy you are in the legal profession. The last major cause of unhappiness for attorneys worth discussing is burnout.

It is important that you know there is a lot of burnout in the legal profession. Some attorneys get burned out on the work that they once loved. Other attorneys realized that they are doing work that they never wanted to do in the first place. Some attorneys get tired of the clients and just don't want to deal with them anymore.

I have seen a lot of attorney burnout, and it is not pretty. An attorney that is burned-out is constantly unhappy and constantly complaining. They are unhappy about their practice, their career, and pretty much everything. One attorney I know is so unhappy that other attorneys don't like to be around her. People don't get burned-out overnight. It happens slowly and usually takes month if not years. Burnout doesn't have to be inevitable and there are some things you can do to avoid burnout.

When you are young, try out different areas of law to see what you like and what you enjoy. Some young attorneys think they would hate criminal law, but when they try it they end up loving it. If you try an area of law and you hate it that's OK too. It is better to try something and realize that you don't like it than to never discover an area of law that you could have enjoyed. Think of this as when your mom made you eat some food you didn't want to and she told you just had to try it once.

Another good idea is to talk to attorneys that have been practicing for a while in the area of law you are interested in. You may think you are interested in family law until you talk to some family law attorneys. The more attorneys you speak to the better idea you will get if the field of law is for you. It is not a bad idea to attend some conferences for the field of law you are interested in. If you are interested in immigration law find a local conference and go to it. This is a great way to meet many attorneys in one field of law all at once.

Something else that is very important to remember is that money will not make you happy. There is nothing wrong with wanting to make money. I believe it is easier to be comfortable with money than without it. I have been very poor and not being poor is better. Wanting to make money is different than thinking money will make you happy. Whenever a study or survey is done asking people what makes them happy the answer is never money. The answer is always friends and family. I know lots of attorneys that make lots of money and are as far from happy as you can imagine. If you are unhappy without money you will be unhappy with money. I think money can make a happy person happier, but money can't make an unhappy person happy.

"More money more problems, more problems more money."
— Young Jeezy

A young attorney must also remember that the more work you take on the more stress you will have. There is nothing wrong with taking on a lot of work but you must be aware that this will create more stress and more headaches. Your goal should be to find a good balance between making the amount of money you want and the amount of stress you can handle. If you have too much stress this is not good. If you do not have enough work this will also lead to stress.

Having said that money will not make you happy it would not be honest of me to not add that money is incredibly important. I believe that it is easier to be happy with money than without. Money affords us a lot of luxuries that are impossible without money. There are benefits such as a nice house, nice vacations, good insurance, and many other material luxuries.

Material luxuries do not have to be expensive. For me having a reliable car is a luxury that money buys. When I started my practice I had an old Honda that had a ton of miles on it. I remember driving into my garage in the Phoenix summer and smoke coming out of the engine. Now that I can afford a new car I don't have to worry about my car breaking down. Something as simple as a dependable car is not possible without money.

A more important luxury that money buys is time. If you have money you can choose to work as much or as little as you want. You can take long vacations and be with family. You can go into the office whenever you want or not go in at all. How many people go into the office every day and worry about getting laid off or fired? When you have enough money to walk away from your job or your practice you do not have that concern. Many of the older attorneys that I know did not save enough money for retirement and are forced to work longer than they would like to. If you have enough money you can choose to retire and do whatever you want. The bottom line is that money buys you choices.

Another important role that money plays is that it allows you to enjoy your work more. None of us would want to work as ditch diggers because the work is hard and does not pay well. Now imagine if I offered you a ditch-digging job that pays $10,000 a day. Suddenly you have a different outlook on the job. The same idea holds true for attorneys. Today I am doing essentially the same work that I was doing three years ago. The difference is now I am making close to four times the money I was three years ago. Guess if I am happier going to work today or three years ago. When you are making good money (however you define good) it is easier waking up in the morning and going into the office. When I talk to my public defender friends their biggest complaint is that they are not being paid enough. If their salary were doubled I guarantee they would enjoy waking up on Monday mornings a lot more. As in most things in life balance is key.

Having Small and Large Things to Look Forward To

You must have things in your life that you look forward to. Having things that you are looking forward to will help you get through the rough times and the stressful things. For a lot of people vacations are something that they look forward to. I know attorneys that plan trips years out just so they can look forward to them. The thing that you look forward to doesn't have to be a vacation; it could be a purchase or anything else. The thing that you are looking forward to also doesn't have to be large. The thing that you look forward to can be going to the movies with your significant other or going to the gym at the end of the day to help you unwind. A big part of unwinding is taking time off.

Young attorneys must remember to take time off work. Make time for family, vacations, social outings, and anything else that you enjoy. Obviously, when you are starting out you will be taking fewer vacations and days off than once you are established but you must make time for yourself. If do not make time for yourself you will get burned-out. Taking time off can be sleeping in one morning or taking half the day off and going home to take a nap. The entire point of having your own practice is to be able to enjoy things more and do things on your own schedule.

I started this chapter with a quote from one of my favorite TV shows *The Wire*. The quote is being said to a detective that is obsessed with his work and willing to go to all ends to get the bad guy. The wise detective friend tells him that "the job will not save him."

What the quote means is that people need to have more in their lives than work. No matter how good you are at your job, no matter how busy you are you must have more than work. Work can bring you happiness but not on the same level as family and friends. You need hobbies, families, activities, volunteer causes and things you care about besides work. I have seen attorneys that have nothing in their lives aside from work and it is not something to aspire to. You must have balance. Work hard, spend a lot of time working, but have balance.

Finding Balance

I have attorney friends that find balance in different ways. I have one attorney friend who has a condo in San Diego and drives there a couple times a month. I have friends who have cabins and spend as much time there as possible. Other attorneys stay in town but volunteer a lot at animal shelters or other worthy causes. I have one attorney friend who spends every weekend at various shelters trying to find homes for abandoned animals. For her, there is no better way to spend the weekend. I like to travel and try to have date night with my wife every Saturday. For me having planned trips is important because it gives me something big to look forward to. It doesn't matter what you do to get away from work, but there has to be more to your life than work.

Another important part of finding balance has nothing to do with your practice. If you do not surround yourself with people that make you happy your life will be out of balance. I know attorneys that have balance in their work but don't have balance in their marriages and they are unhappy. If your practice is going well but you are miserable in your marriage what are the chances that you will be happy? If you are up all night arguing with your significant other, how effective will you be in court the next morning? This is not a relationship-help book, but remember that if your home life is not happy this will affect your work life.

Saving Your Money

Lawyers, and most professionals, have a choice they have to make early on in their careers. They choice is, Do you want to have real wealth later on or pretend to have wealth now? My definition of real wealth is being able to stop working and not worrying about money. Unless your parents have left you a wildly successful law firm, or you have done well in drug dealing, chances are you will not have a lot of money when you start your own practice. Not only will you not have a lot of money when you start, you won't have a lot of money for a number of years.

Eventually you will start to make a little bit of money and this is when you will have to choose. You can either invest or save the money, or you can spend it right away.

Spending every last dollar and pretending to have wealth is what most lawyers do. It is hard to blame them because we live in a consumer culture where everyone wants to have the newest everything. Many people measure their self-worth based on the things they buy. If you choose this option, you will never achieve real wealth and real financial independence. Your entire career you will continue to spend money and never acquire assets that will make money for you. I know many lawyers that chose this option and now regret it because they wish they could afford to retire but they cannot. To me there are few things sadder than someone who has worked hard their whole life and has very little financial success to show for it. I recently spoke with an older attorney that told me at one point when his practice was going well he had spent close to $50,000 on home electronics. He told me how badly he wished he had saved that money and how much better off he would be now had he saved and invested that money.

I know an amazing number of lawyers that make a lot of money but don't save any of it. I know lawyers that live from paycheck to paycheck and will do so for their entire lives. These lawyers own many flashy things, which they brag about and show off. These lawyers chose to have pretend wealth.

The second option is harder but will pay off in the long run. If you invest or save the money you will have the opportunity to achieve real wealth later on in life. You will have to plan and save and invest your money and this is less fun in the short term. While your friends are buying new cars or boats you are putting money in a retirement account. While your friends take out home equity loans and buy expensive jewelry you are buying rental property. I understand there is a sacrifice but it is a sacrifice with a purpose.

Think of any world-class athlete and how much they sacrifice to get to where they are. While an athlete's friends are partying and eating junk food the athlete is training and counting calories. The athlete has a goal and knows what they must do to achieve it. The athlete knows the payoff will be worth the sacrifice. Investing in your financial future is the same idea.

To achieve real wealth you will have to sacrifice in the short term, but you will be better off in the long run. When you are older and ready to stop working you will have that option. This does not mean you have to stop working but that you have the choice. Remember that one of the main reasons you probably started your own practice in the first place was to give yourself choices. Just remember to ask yourself if you want real wealth later or pretend wealth now.

Taking Care of Your Health

All the success in the world means nothing if you are sick or dead. This is a grim, but important, lesson for lawyers that own their own practices. To build a successful practice you have to work hard and you have to work hard for a long time. Sometimes the hard work and long hours can have an effect on a lawyer's health. I have seen this many times myself where a lawyer will let their health deteriorate. I hear a lot of things like "I would go to the gym but I am too busy."

If you build the most successful practice in the history of business but you are too sick to enjoy any of the fruits of your labor, what is the point? One of my closest mentors died from poor health at 38. He was not only my mentor but also a close friend. My friend had a thriving practice and was doing incredibly well. He was on his way to being one of the most successful lawyers in town. He had a loving wife and small kids. He loved being a lawyer and was very good at it. While he was busy working his health started slipping away from him. He gained a lot of weight, didn't eat well, and didn't exercise. He also didn't take vacations because he said there was no time. He was a workaholic and often worked seven days a week.

One day he got the flu, the flu turned into bronchitis, that turned into a blood clot, and after being sick for a couple of weeks he died. He had built an awesome practice and had everything in the world to look forward to but he was dead. I know that if he had been in better health his body would have had a better chance of pulling through. I always think of my friend when I am debating putting off a vacation or working out. Your health should always come before your work. You should know your cholesterol, blood pressure, and other important vitals. Sticking your head in the sand and hoping everything is OK is not an acceptable approach.

The bottom line is simple. You have to take care of your health. No matter how busy you are you always have time to eat healthy and get in some exercise. Exercise will not only improve your health but will help you to deal with stress. Everything is tied to everything so if your health is better, your mood is better, the less stress you have and so on. The opposite is also true. The worse health you are in, the less exercise you get, the worse your mood gets and so on.

You don't have to be a marathon runner to get exercise. Take fifteen minutes and walk around your office building or take your dog for a walk. It is not important what you do for exercise or how strenuous it is. As long as you are doing anything that involves moving there will be a benefit. Getting exercise is not only good for your stress level but also you will have more energy and be able to work more. Exercising is important and so is taking time off. Simple things like walking around the block can be helpful.

If you don't know how to start, there are plenty of people that can help. If you don't know how to work out, get a personal trainer. If you don't know how to eat healthy get a nutritionist. If your back hurts find a chiropractor. If your excuse is that you can't afford these people you need a better excuse. Saving money is great but not when it comes to your health. Also don't forget to think of the long-term benefits of spending money on your health. Spending a couple of hundred dollars on a nutritionist now could save you tens of thousands of dollars in medical and insurance bills down the road. I am always amazed when a lawyer is willing to spend $60,000 on a new car but not $600 on a personal trainer.

I know parts of this book may not be exactly optimistic but I feel it is better that you start thinking about things that many attorneys choose not to think about like financial independence and taking care of your health. The topics covered in this book are topics that all law practice owners have to deal with. The choice you have to make is: Do you want to think about these issues now or when they spring up on you down the road? In all honesty the practice of law has been amazing to me. I have been able to do amazing things and make a good living in the process. For all the complaining about difficult clients and the other problems in the legal profession there is truly nothing else I would rather do. The practice of law has been good to me and I hope it will be just as good to you. I feel I am incredibly fortunate to have the job and career that I have.

So far having my own practice has worked out incredibly well for me. When I was starting out I could not have dreamt of the opportunities that my practice has presented to me. It sounds like a cliché but I really do feel incredibly lucky to be able to do what I do and to make what I make. I love not having to answer to anyone and to make my own rules. As I said in the beginning of this book, being able to chart my own path means everything to me. I hope having your own practice will be as great for you as it has been for me. If anything in this book is useful to you in your legal journey I will be happy. Remember that having your practice is not easy but nothing worth doing ever is. BEST OF LUCK!

Index